PENGUIN PASSNOTES

Oral English for GCSE

Vivian Summers was educated at the universities of Exeter and Cambridge. He has been Head of the English Department at a large West Country comprehensive school and has lectured at a College of Education. He holds professional qualifications in speech and has for many years taught, examined and written about Spoken English. He has been appointed a visiting assessor in the subject for one of the GCSE Examining Groups and he is an examiner for the English Speaking Board, of which he is a Fellow. He is also a freelance writer with several books on English to his credit.

PENGUIN PASSNOTES

VIVIAN SUMMERS

Oral English for GCSE

ADVISORY EDITOR: S. H. COOTE, M.A., PH.D.

PENGUIN BOOKS

Penguin Books Ltd, Harmondsworth, Middlesex, England
Viking Penguin Inc., 40 West 23rd Street, New York, New York 10010, U.S.A.
Penguin Books Australia Ltd, Ringwood, Victoria, Australia
Penguin Books Canada Ltd, 2801 John Street, Markham, Ontario, Canada L3R 1B4
Penguin Books (N.Z.) Ltd, 182–190 Wairau Road, Auckland 10, New Zealand

First published 1987

Made and printed in Great Britain by
Richard Clay Ltd, Bungay, Suffolk
Typeset in Monophoto Ehrhardt

Contents

Introduction

'Not just an exam – more a way of life'

According to the regulations, you cannot be awarded a GCSE certificate in English unless you have gained at least a Grade 5 in Oral English, which will be assessed separately from the written papers.

You might think from this that two courses will be running in your English class – one for written and one for oral English – and that the two subjects are quite distinct. Nothing could be further from the truth. The subject which you are studying and which will be assessed concerns the use of the English language in its four aspects of reading, writing, listening and speaking. Although it is convenient to assess speaking (and with it listening) on its own, it is an integral part of the whole English course. When you ask or answer a question in class, when you talk about the play or novel you are reading, when you work in a group on a project or have a group discussion, you are using oral English as part of the normal work of the classroom. It enables you to get things done. Without it, the project would never be started, the scene based on the novel would never be improvised and lively exchanges of ideas would never take place. *Oral English is not something special*, invented by examiners. It is a principal tool – perhaps *the* principal tool – for work in the classroom. As it says above, we are talking about 'not just an exam – more a way of life'.

So important is this use of the spoken language that the Examination Groups agree that it should be part of your GCSE assessment. (After all, a subject can't be neglected if it is a compulsory part of an examination syllabus!) Therefore the way you use spoken English during your two-year course will be assessed and given a grade which will appear on your GCSE certificate. It will not be too difficult to achieve that Grade 5 which will entitle you to collect the English certificate (providing you have a Grade G for the written part). But you will obviously not be satisfied with the bare minimum. Your certificate should record the best standard you are capable of and the advice in this book is designed to help you achieve it.

Getting things done

You usually speak to get things done. Planning a shopping expedition, finding out what the family want for dinner, agreeing who is to use the car or what TV programme is to be watched are a very few examples of the countless ways we use speech in our everyday lives. Similarly in the classroom we use speech to organize projects, arrange group activities, discuss questions we are to write about with fellow students and the teacher. This kind of speech is now being called 'talk as process' – which simply means talk which arises out of an activity and is not an end in itself. This kind of talk has to be assessed in GCSE.

Talk for talk's sake

Another kind of talk is when the end-product is talk itself. An obvious example of this is a speech delivered at a public meeting. Less obviously, a discussion in a pub about the local football team is another example. These are cases when people are talking for no other reason than the interest and pleasure of the talk itself. This is known as 'talk as product'. In the classroom examples of this would be holding a discussion on a topic of current affairs, making up a dramatic scene, reading aloud, improvising a telephone conversation or giving a short talk. In each example the end-product *is* the talking. GCSE candidates must be given opportunities to show their abilities in this kind of 'talk as product' as well as 'talk as process'.

Assessing your achievement

There are so many kinds of talk and of speech situations that you would feel it unfair to be assessed on one occasion only – on a fateful examination day when you could be off-colour or shattered by nerves. To overcome this, the Examination Groups require candidates to be given a large element of continuous assessment. This is similar to the coursework which is a feature of most GCSE written examinations. Two of the Groups require continuous assessment *and* a special end-of-course oral test, but the other three rely entirely on continuous assessment. (Your school may decide that a special test or, more probably, a series of tests spread through the course could be helpful as part of its continuous assessment of your oral achievement.)

Who are the oral examiners?

The examiners are the same people who will be assessing your written work during the course and marking the final exams – in other words, your own teachers. There are very detailed regulations, set down by the Examining Groups, about how they are to assess you, and the teachers will be attending special meetings to ensure that their standards are the same as those of other schools. External moderators may visit the school to see a sample of work in progress and to inspect records of what you have achieved. Everything will be done to ensure that the standards of oral assessing methods are up to the requirements of an important public examination.

Who chooses the activities?

Your teachers will not only be the assessors: they will also be responsible for choosing the speech activities in which you take part through the course. They have to follow the regulations and make sure that you are given the chance to develop and show your achievement in a variety of oral situations. They must also make sure that you have ample opportunity to use talk both as 'process' and as 'product'.

Seeing that your teachers have the great responsibility of directing your oral activities and also assessing them, it is reasonable to expect them to explain to you at the outset (and to remind you from time to time) how they will be carrying out the assessments. You should also be told the name of the Examining Group whose syllabus you are following and whether or not there is to be an end-of-course test. For those Examining Groups who do require such a test, your teacher will be able to tell you precisely what is required and how to prepare for it. Giving a talk and taking part in a discussion are likely to figure prominently.

You should remember that useful talk is part of the everyday life of an English classroom, and your readiness to contribute orally to the work of the class will be noted by your teacher and will influence his or her overall assessment of you. In other words, do not think that your final grade will be based solely on those occasions when the teacher has let you know that an assessment is taking place. Very often opportunities for spoken English will be linked with the other main activities of reading and writing: you may not be aware that you are 'doing' oral English at all!

In this book, while recognizing the integrated nature of English work, we shall be looking at several kinds of speech activities in turn. The aim is to help you to raise your standard in each of them. The result should be more than a good grade in oral English: it should assist you to talk effectively in the world that lies beyond school – which is the real point of this part of your English course.

The Oral Syllabuses

The syllabuses for English issued by the five Examination Boards in England and Wales are long and detailed. The sections on oral English usually cover several pages; they contain advice to the teachers on the kind of work that the GCSE hopes to encourage as well as instructions on assessment procedures. To give you an idea of the approach adopted by each Examining Board and the sort of activities they expect you to meet during your English course, here is a short digest of the requirements of each Board. It is *not* the complete official syllabus; this can be obtained from the Board in question.

London and East Anglian Group

This Board requires (a) a final coursework mark and also (b) a mark for a group oral test to be taken at the end of the spring term of the examination year.

(a) *Coursework*: it is expected that several activities would take place during the course and be assessed. These could include formal and informal discussions, talks given to large or small groups, role-play, scripted drama and improvisation, interviews, practice in reading aloud prose and verse.

(b) *Group oral test*: groups of 5 or 6 candidates will be examined together. Each will give a talk on a subject of his or her own choice, lasting three or four minutes, and this will be followed by a group discussion after each talk lasting about five minutes.

Midland Examining Group

Each candidate will be assessed on five different speech activities undertaken during the course. The Board does not prescribe what these must be but gives several examples of the kind of work that might be assessed. These include small group discussions; introducing a topic for discussion; chairing a meeting; formal debate; role-play; reading aloud and play-reading; prepared talks; focused conversation with teacher; giving instructions; reporting back; giving an account of something learnt recently.

Northern Examining Association

Assessment will be based on a wide variety of activities undertaken during the course. These might include a talk, a reading, role-play, a report, an interview, narration of an anecdote, an explanation, etc. Oral work would also arise within the context of other English class activities and these might include discussion of a poem, a story or a topic; preparing a list of questions; brainstorming; preparing a statement of findings; solving a problem; interviewing, etc.

Southern Examining Group

This Group expects the teacher to provide as many opportunities as he or she wishes for candidates to take part in oral work for assessment. It requires candidates to be assessed within three contexts: (a) pair work in which two people collaborate on a specified task, (b) open-ended group discussion for four people, and (c) an individual exposition given by the candidate to an audience of one or more persons. This might involve introducing a discussion topic, reporting back, explaining the use of a piece of equipment or a process, explaining an operation or a phenomenon, narrating a story, relating an experience, presenting an argument, preparing a motion in a debate.

Welsh Joint Education Committee

There will be (a) a coursework mark based on a wide range of evidence, including specifically designed oral tasks and also the candidate's contribution to the day-to-day work of the English class, and (b) an end-of-course mark based on one or more situations specifically devised for assessment purposes. The Board uses broad categories of formal and semi-formal speech situations, though acknowledging that there are degrees of formality within an individual speech situation. It gives several examples of both categories for the guidance of teachers. The formal activities include group discussion with a chairman; reporting to the class the outcome of a group discussion; a prepared talk to the class, followed by questions; debate; simulation of a formal interview. The semi-formal activities include group discussion in a semi-formal style – recounting an anecdote, describing an event, discussing a book, story or poem which has been read or a play which has been seen, etc.; improvised acting situations; one-to-one conversation arising from a project or topic of interest to the candidate; contribution to class discussions.

The syllabuses of the Northern Ireland Schools Examinations Council for GCSE and of the Scottish Examination Board for the Scottish Certificate of Education are on similar lines.

The details given above are nothing more than a summary of the oral activities suggested by the Examination Groups to teachers as being suitable for assessment. The teachers within individual schools will be responsible for choosing the activities they wish their students to undertake during the GCSE course. Do not think that you personally will have to take part in every single activity listed here!

All the Groups in their full syllabuses stress the inter-relatedness of all the aspects of English work and the great importance they attach to *listening* as well as speaking.

Although there are individual differences in the suggestions given by the Groups, you will notice the frequent mention of the following: group discussions (with or without a chairman), reporting back, interviews, giving a talk followed by questions and discussion, telling a story, debating, introducing a passage and reading it aloud, role-play. All these speech activities are discussed in this book.

Discussion

The most common form of talk is discussion. The word covers a very wide range of speech activities. Within a family it varies from a brief exchange between parent and child about who is to cut the grass up to a large family conference to plan a summer holiday or to discuss the wedding arrangements of a grown-up daughter. At work it may be a few remarks between the foreman and a workman about how a job is to be carried out or a full-blown boardroom conference about the future of a company. At the highest international level it would include a summit meeting of world leaders.

Mostly discussion is intended to resolve a problem or plan a course of action. Sometimes, however, a discussion can simply be an airing of views, pursued for its own sake and for the interest of the participants. Examples of this would be talk between friends about the fortunes of a sports team and arguments over the pros and cons of a political programme.

The GCSE Examination Boards regard discussion as a principal activity within the classroom and the kind of talk nearest to real life. They therefore expect teachers to give you opportunities for discussions of different kinds during your course. The assessment of your achievement in these will provide a substantial element in your final grading in oral English. You may be told by your teacher that assessment will be carried out during a certain discussion, but it would be wise to assume from the beginning of your two-year GCSE course that you may be assessed at any time and on many occasions – just as all your written work may be considered for coursework assessment. Remember that the final assessment in Oral English will not be based on a single test, but will be a composite grade derived from the several opportunities you will have had for using spoken English in class.

The number of people taking part in a discussion will vary

according to circumstances. It may be as few as two people working together to plan a project or as many as five or six. (Beyond this number the group becomes unwieldy – certainly for classroom purposes – and many of the participants just sit and listen to two or three principal speakers.) This kind of talk is called *Group Discussion* and all those within the group have the chance to play an equal part – though not all may take it!

But there is another kind of discussion, also well known in the world beyond school. This is the *interview*. This differs from group discussion in two ways. First of all, it usually involves only two people, so that each participant is bound to contribute substantially to the discussion if it is to succeed at all. The second difference is that one of the participants very often holds a position of authority which the other recognizes and adjusts to. An example of this is a job interview, where one person is the employer with the power to award a job and the other is the applicant anxious to receive it.

GROUP DISCUSSION

There are so many kinds of group discussion likely to occur in the classroom that it is impossible to analyse each in turn. What follows here is advice applicable to most discussions and designed to help you improve your personal contribution to the work of the group.

Be ready to talk, but . . .

Imagine two people within a group of five discussing the rights and wrongs of blood sports. The first begins to talk straight away, speaks at length, hardly allows anyone else to get a word in edgeways and ends up thinking he has made a dazzling contribution to the discussion. The second person sits still, with head down, allows the torrent of speech to flow over him and never says a word from the beginning to the end of the discussion. Each of these two has been equally disastrous as a member of a group discussion. The first has turned the discussion into a selfish monologue; the second might as well have not been present.

The essence of discussion is a readiness to share ideas and to listen to what others have to say. The silent member may have been listening to what his colleagues had to say, but it made no difference to his contribution because he did not say anything himself. Listening is important but it has to be made use of. When you are placed in a discussion group, work on the assumption that your opinions and ideas are as valuable as the next person's and that if you do not put them forward the group will have lost something worth hearing.

Gaining confidence

Taking a full part in a group discussion is very often a matter of confidence. Some people find no difficulty in expressing their views; others just clam up when the talking begins. If you are one of the latter you will find it easier to join in conversation if you have made some preparations beforehand. Presumably you will have been given some warning that a discussion will take place on a certain topic and that your ideas will be welcomed. You therefore have the chance for some quiet thinking or even research before the group meets. Think of two or three points that you could use in the forthcoming discussion and write them down. This forces you to be quite definite about what you have in mind. If possible, think of an example or illustration to go with each point and jot this down as well. Now you will approach the discussion armed with something definite to say and this alone should give you the courage to put your points forward. This is not meant to suggest that you would read your points out from your notes. Keep the paper in your pocket, but have the points available in your mind. If another speaker 'steals' one of your points by mentioning it before you do, you can still enter the discussion with such a remark as, 'I agree with that. I also think that . . .' and you can support the point in your own words. What is more, you could then bring forward the illustration you had prepared in support. Once you have spoken, you will find it much easier to come into the conversation again . . . and again.

Open-ended talk

Many discussions are undertaken for their own sake – to examine issues, exchange ideas, and clarify opinions. This is 'Talk as product' which was mentioned in the Introduction (p. 8). This kind of discussion has a life of its own. When you take part in it, you do not know how and where it will end. It may quite naturally turn away from the original topic because the group as a whole find a new aspect more rewarding to explore. For example, the group may be discussing seal-clubbing (the method of keeping down the number of seals by clubbing baby seals to death). The discussion may concentrate more and more on Man's general responsibility towards animals which share his environment. The particular question about how to control the seal population has been overtaken by a broader topic that arose directly from it. This is not a case of being irrelevant and going off the point: the original subject has been widened and made more generally applicable. This is what happens in a good discussion and it would be a pity if someone said, 'Well, we'd better get back to the baby seals'. Such a remark would show that the speaker did not realize how a discussion can develop.

Talk with a purpose

The kind of discussion which is intended to lead to something being done – such as a project being carried out, an expedition arranged or a piece of drama being presented – is known as 'talk as process', also mentioned in the Introduction (p. 8). Here the talk is part of a planning process and members of the group have to keep in mind what they are hoping to achieve by it. The discussion certainly may open up areas not at first in the minds of the participants, but it is important that the group does not lose sight of its aim. If you are making arrangements for an outing with the sailing club, it may be very tempting for the group to talk about the time last year when somebody's boat capsized – one such reminiscence can quickly lead to another. But that is not helping with the planning of the present expedition and so the person who says, 'We'd better get back to this year's plans' will be doing a useful job.

Starting a discussion

Someone has to start a discussion and it could well be you. There are distinct advantages in being the first to speak. What you say is very likely to indicate the direction the discussion will take, although it may change and develop as things go on. But your remark will have been the starting point and, unless the second speaker brushes it aside completely, you will have seized the initiative. Try to make your point positive and of sufficient length to be fully understood. You should aim to stimulate a response, even if it is an opposing point of view. Here are some possible openings to the discussion on seal-clubbing. What do you think of them?

1. Well, I don't agree with it. It's cruel.
2. I saw it on television the other night. It made me feel sick.
3. People who do that ought to be clubbed themselves.
4. It said on TV that seal-clubbing is necessary to protect the stocks of fish in the sea. Perhaps that's true, but I don't think Man should interfere with the balance of Nature.

The first three examples are unsuccessful as starters to a discussion. No. 1 makes a very brief emotional statement and leaves it at that. No. 2 gives a personal reaction that may be honest but leads nowhere. No. 3's response is crude and unproductive. Only in No. 4 do we have a remark which contains points that can lead the discussion forward – for example, have we the right to kill seals to protect our own food supplies; should Man ever interfere with the balance of Nature? It would now be up to someone else in the group to respond to this lead, taking up one of the possible openings and adding something to it. In this way the discussion would be off to a good start.

Developing a discussion

There are several ways in which you can play your part in developing the discussion once the initial remark has been made. Here are six of them:

1. Supporting a remark that has just been made by stating your agreement with it and adding an illustration of your own as evidence.
2. Supplying a new point, with supporting evidence, which will reinforce the direction which the discussion is already taking.
3. Challenging a remark just made and offering an argument against it. This is a very fruitful contribution because it stops people accepting too easily the prevailing line of the discussion and may sharply divide the group and provoke a lively clash of opinions. A discussion in which everyone thinks the same way quickly becomes boring.
4. Putting a question to one of the previous speakers. This may not amount to a challenge, as in No. 3, but it may encourage the speaker to explain himself or herself more clearly. This might then provoke agreement or disagreement.
5. Intervening to clarify or summarize the argument so far. This would be necessary if you felt the discussion was becoming confused and therefore no progress was being made. It would help everybody if a member of the group attempted to sum up and then to suggest how the discussion could move forward. This is not an easy thing to do, but is worth trying – and would be well rewarded if an assessment were taking place.
6. Providing evidence for or against an argument that someone else has put forward.

Getting into an argument . . .

If you are a member of a lively group in which everybody is anxious to speak you may find it difficult to intervene to raise the point you have in mind. It will be easier if you have a few phrases on the tip of your tongue which can be used to introduce your remarks. If you want to speak in support of something that has just been said, these phrases will be useful:

1. I agree with that and think that . . .
2. That's quite true, and . . .

3. I think (Tom's) right about that. I believe that . . .
4. Perhaps we ought to consider too . . .

In each case, the phrase enables you to go on and introduce your own point in support.

You may want to oppose, rather than support, the previous argument. You therefore could use such phrases as:

1. I'm afraid I don't agree with that. It seems to me that . . .
2. Well, yes, but on the other hand . . .
3. That may be so, but . . .
4. But surely we have to consider . . .
5. That's all very well, but . . .
6. You may be right up to a point, but . . .

. . . And keeping cool

You will have noticed that every one of those six remarks begins with a phrase that in some way or other softens the impact of your opposition. Nos. 2, 3 and 6 actually seem to be partly agreeing with the previous speaker and No. 1 is apologizing for not being able to go along with the argument. All this is for the purpose of keeping the argument pleasant and friendly, even when there may be sharp differences of opinion. It is very easy to take disagreement with your point of view as a personal insult and to feel resentment against your opponent – especially if he or she is getting the better of the argument! This spoils the discussion for everybody and little progress will be made if people lose their tempers. So do your part in keeping the exchanges relaxed and courteous and look for ways of defusing any potentially dangerous comments from others. Above all, avoid 'personalities': that is to say, remarks which attack, not views, but the persons who express them.

Listening

The person who talks non-stop is unlikely to be very successful in a discussion group. Apart from the fact that he or she makes it very difficult for others to contribute, that kind of person can gain nothing from the views of others. A good talker should also be a good listener. Real progress is made in a discussion if the members listen carefully and thoughtfully to what each individual is saying and then use what they have heard when they put forward their own points. These may be agreeing or disagreeing with the arguments of others, but their remarks will be modified by what other members of the group are saying. This will lead either to an eventual consensus of opinion or else to an 'agreement to differ', with all sides of the case well understood. If you do not listen to the others, none of this will be possible.

If an assessor is present during the discussion, he or she will be looking for evidence of good *listening* and will give credit for it. You may wonder how anyone can know how a candidate is actually listening to what is being said. It is not too difficult and you can try it out for yourself when you have the chance to observe a discussion group in action. Look at the expressions on the faces of those who are not speaking. Are they bored and inattentive or are they following with their eyes each speaker in turn? Are they nodding their heads in agreement sometimes? Are they smiling or showing by other facial expressions their reactions to what is going on? All these are signs that active listening is taking place.

Good listening is essential but it has to be made use of. It is possible that just occasionally you may have little to say in a discussion, preferring to listen with interest to what the others are talking about, but usually you make use of your listening when you next have your say – and this is the best evidence that you *have* been listening. A successful member of a discussion group is someone who can pick up the points already made and use them for his or her own purposes to support or refute, to develop or modify.

The spoilers

There are several ways of wrecking a discussion and they are often used by people who think they are doing rather well! Here are some imaginary portraits of students who would *not* rate highly in discussion.

George likes the sound of his own voice. He is a fluent talker, even though he does not think much before he speaks. He is always the first to open a discussion and when he gets into his stride it is difficult to stop him. When another member does get a word in edgeways, George listens impatiently for a few seconds, grunting the while to keep his energy in check, and then he breaks in again before the other speaker has finished. If someone makes a really determined attempt to speak, George counters this by raising his voice and speaking even faster. At the end of the discussion, George is confident that he has done very well indeed. The assessor thinks otherwise.

Janet is something like George, but her approach is more subtle. She too finds it easy to dominate a discussion but her method does not rely on endless talk. On the contrary, she goes out of her way to allow others to talk – by appointing herself chairwoman! Nobody asks her to take on this job nor wants her to, but Janet enjoys her self-appointed eminence. After an opening statement, she remarks, 'Now, Mary, what do you think?' This is quite helpful in bringing Mary into the discussion and no one would complain if Janet left it at that. But she doesn't. 'Do you agree with that, John?' she asks briskly; when John has responded she turns to Bill for his opinion, and then to Susan and so on around the group. The result is that no one feels free to speak unless Janet asks them to. No real discussion takes place – only a series of questions and answers controlled by Janet. Like George, she feels she has done a very good job. In actual fact she has ruined the discussion for everyone.

Susan is another who can speak fairly easily, but not in discussion groups. Serious discussion tends to bore her and listening and thinking are rather an effort. However, she sometimes finds an opening when she can really enjoy herself and others in the group follow her lead all too readily. *Susan likes to chat.* It may be that the group is discussing modern developments in the retail trade – the value of hyper-markets, the changes in department stores and the dwindling number of village shops. Susan sees her chance: 'You can get lovely clothes down at the market,' she says. 'Last Saturday I bought a new skirt there for only six pounds . . .' Fatally, others will follow her lead and the discussion will deteriorate into pointless chatting about where to buy clothes and how to save money when you go shopping in town.

John is not much help either, though he does try. He pays attention to what is going on – up to a point. Unfortunately he tends to stick with that one point only and not to notice when the discussion has moved beyond it. Let's say the topic being considered is 'Space travel and its value'. John is very impressed with the idea that in years to come the human race may need to find another planet to live on. This is discussed very fully and then the group moves on to discuss whether space travel is really worth the millions and millions spent on it. Just when the discussion is moving forward to yet another point, John intervenes firmly: 'Yes and I think Mankind will have to think about living on another planet one day.' Back to square one. John has spoiled the forward movement of the discussion, re-opened a point already considered and lost the new point that was just emerging.

You would be very unlucky to be in a group containing people like these, but they do exist – the overbearing talker, the self-appointed chairman, the chatty gossiper and the arguer in circles. There are other kinds of spoilers too, such as the people who contribute remarks of only five or six words before relapsing into silence, the mumblers whose words are difficult to hear anyway and the very silent ones who are not even listening properly. It might be worth asking yourself if any of these people could just possibly be – you!

As a contrast to all these negative characteristics which can spoil a discussion, here are some of the qualities that mark out the successful member of a group. He or she would be able to:

1. Introduce new points clearly and supply supporting evidence, speaking at a reasonable length.
2. Develop a point put forward by another speaker.
3. Challenge courteously a point of view he or she did not agree with.
4. Ask relevant questions to clarify an issue.
5. Draw out a shy member of the group without appearing to dominate.

6. Respond to a change in the direction of the discussion.
7. Draw together the threads of a discussion when it seems useful to come to a conclusion.
8. Use examples and personal experience to illustrate points of general application.
9. Be aware of other people in the group, allowing them to have their say and taking account of their views.
10. Speak clearly with appropriate vocabulary and style of language.

Being a chairman

So far we have been talking about discussion groups in which all members are on equal terms, but sometimes it is convenient to have an officially appointed chairman. If you are asked to fill this position, what would you have to do?

Your principal task is to enable the discussion to proceed as smoothly and as efficiently as possible. For this purpose you are unlikely to speak a great deal yourself. Your job is to allow others to have their say. Before the talking begins, weigh up who are the members of the group. You will probably know already that there are two or three extroverts who will try to take over the proceedings and three others who are prepared to let them! Controlling the talkative and bringing out the quiet ones will be up to you.

At the start you will state the subject you have been asked to discuss. If there is any uncertainty about what this means precisely, you will explain your understanding of the topic by way of introduction and then invite those present to give their views. It is possible that your introduction may be a formal speech which you have prepared for assessment and then you go on to act as chairman of the discussion which your talk has stimulated. This way of initiating a discussion is very much in line with the thinking behind the examination syllabuses. Once the time for discussion has come, you will need to deploy the skills of a chairman, unless you are specifically instructed otherwise.

In order to start the discussion, it is better not to name an individual and ask for his or her opinion. Let the discussion develop as naturally as possible and keep your own interventions to the minimum. If two people begin to talk at exactly the same time, then you should name one of them, giving that person the right to speak. If the other speaker will not give way, then you must assert your authority as chairman and insist that speakers abide by your ruling.

Let the discussion ebb and flow in its own way and – providing it is not getting hopelessly confused – do not try to restrict it to one narrow line of development. Fruitful discussion will often grow away from its original starting point. On the other hand, if you have been given a very clear assignment on which some kind of conclusion has to be reached and reported back to the class or to the teacher, then you will have to remind the group of this if it seems to be wandering too far off the point. Never allow the group just to chat!

Helping really shy members is not easy: you do not want to embarrass them and so cause them to shrink into their shells even more. A breezy remark such as 'Come on, Helen, you haven't opened your mouth all the morning', is likely to be unproductive. It is better to wait until there is a point on which you think Helen might be able to comment and then say quietly something like, 'Helen, what do you think about that?' or 'I think you know something about that, Helen.' What you should *not* say is, 'Do you agree with that, Helen?' This will simply enable Helen to say either yes or no and not another word more. Therefore avoid questions which require only a yes or no answer. Try to phrase your encouraging question in such a way that the response must be at least a sentence long.

Be careful that you do not establish the habit of asking everyone in turn for his or her views, naming them one by one around the circle. This would make you similar to Janet, whom we described among 'The Spoilers' – someone who becomes a kind of question-master, making people speak only in response to the 'chair' and quickly killing off the free exchange of views which is the essence of a group discussion.

What can a chairman do if the discussion completely dies and the members look at each other in silence? Do not be afraid of silence: it often occurs during discussions. Just wait for a short while. It is remarkable how often someone will come forward after a pause with a new point and resurrect the whole discussion. It may well be you who has to supply the fresh start and so, during the pause, you should be thinking of how you could re-launch the proceedings if no one else takes the initiative. How long you should allow the pause to last must be a matter for your own judgement, depending on the group and its attitude; but in some circumstances a pause of thirty seconds or more may not be too long.

What you may have to counter is the member who says firmly after only a five-second pause, 'Well, there's nothing more to say about that, then.' This may well be mental laziness on his or her part and you could reply, 'Let's just see if there isn't one more point we could add.' This keeps the discussion open for a little longer, during which time you or someone else might supply a new idea.

If nothing emerges, you could sum up for the group so far. By doing this, you give the group time to think over what has been said and it is quite possible that the discussion will pick up again when your summary is concluded. Someone may even disagree with your summary and this will provide further material for talk.

It is the chairman's job to keep the peace and so you should never allow members of the group to show bad temper towards each other. If you see this happening, you should intervene at once to cool the situation. A humorous remark is often helpful, or a reminder that the discussion will never get anywhere if people lose their tempers. Be alert if any single member of the group appears to be picked on by one or more other people. Whatever your personal feelings, your job as chairman is to allow all the members of the group to speak their minds freely and confidently – and courteously. This is not always an easy task!

Reporting back

A chairman is very often asked to summarize and report back the discussion to the whole class. Even if you have not been designated chairman, you may be appointed as reporter. In this case you would be an ordinary member of the group during the session, but would have to give a summary afterwards. As chairman or reporter, how do you go about your task?

It is certainly permissible to take notes while the discussion is going forward. You do not need to write down everything you hear; just make a note of each point that seems important in the argument. If the subject has very obviously two sides to it, then you can divide your paper by a line down the middle and put the points 'for' on one side and those 'against' on the other. What you should *not* do is involve the rest of the group in your note-taking, at least not until the very end of the session. It has been known for a reporter to announce at the beginning of the discussion, 'Now, you know that I have got to give a report on this discussion. So what shall I put down first?' The group then rack their brains and one by one dictate to the reporter points for the list. As each person contributes an idea the rest sit silently, feeling that having made one remark they have nothing else to do. When the reporter thinks there is enough to satisfy the teacher, he or she announces, 'That will do. That's quite enough to be going on with.' The members feel that their work is done and either sit in silence or begin to chat. Of course a discussion never takes place at all – and the reporter is entirely to blame.

On the other hand, it is quite permissible for you as chairman or reporter to say to the group, 'We only have a minute or two left before I have to report back to the class. Will you listen to the points I have noted and then tell me if I have left out anything important?' You then read your list, listen to comments about it from the group and make any necessary amendments. You then have the notes which will be the basis for the summary you must deliver.

In reporting back to the whole class or to the teacher what has been said in the discussion you are, in effect, making a short speech. Take the trouble, therefore, to be audible and quite clear in the arrangement of the points. If you simply work through the notes you jotted down in the discussion, your report is likely to be confused, ranging forward and backward over the arguments that came and went. In the short time between the discussion and the reporting back, number the points in order of importance and cut out the ones which only echoed what had already been said. If you have time, re-write the points in the numbered order and use this new list as notes for your talk. It will be quite brief, but try to make it reflect both sides of opinion represented in your group, though you should indicate where the majority feeling lay.

INTERVIEWS

An interview differs from a discussion between two people. The latter implies that the two people are on equal terms and that their talk is open-ended, whereas an interview suggests that there is a specific purpose in the conversation and that the roles of those taking part are different. The purpose of an interview is nearly always for one of the participants to find out more about the other. The most common example is the job interview, in which an employer has been sufficiently impressed by a job application to wish to meet the applicant and discover whether he or she will be suitable for the post available. (You may be asked to 'role-play' this situation in class.)

Another use of the interview comes when you are trying to find information, say, for a project. You may go to visit somebody who has special knowledge of your subject so that you can ask him or her for information and opinions. For example, you may want to talk to an expert wood-carver for your project on 'old crafts' or you want to hear the opinions of a local councillor on the building of a new by-pass road. In these cases, you are the interviewer.

In the context of a GCSE assessment, however, *you* may be the person being interviewed! It is a recognized form of assessment for your teacher to ask you to come and talk with him or her individually. This is a different kind of speech activity from a group discussion and requires different skills. The interview can be useful to an assessor if you find it difficult to play a full part in group discussion. It may be a way in which you can be encouraged to talk more freely. It is possible that two students may be interviewed together, though more than that number would alter the nature of the talk.

Interviewing people

If you are setting out to interview people to find their opinions or to gain information that is not available elsewhere, there is one basic rule – be prepared! It is a waste of everybody's time if you arrange to visit a person with no clear idea about how you expect to handle the interview. Start your preparation by writing down exactly what you want to find out from your visit – and make sure it is something quite specific. The people you approach are likely to fall into two main categories: (a) those who are very busy and are doing you a favour by giving you some of their time and (b) those who have all the time in the world (such as elderly people) and are glad to chat to someone. In each case it is important to be clear in your own mind what you want to find out. The busy person will be grateful for the directness and clearness of your requests and the leisurely person will be steered by you away from unproductive gossip towards the genuine information you seek. This is not to say that you should rush into an interview, pin your victim into a chair and fire questions at him. You must judge the pace at which the interviewee wants to move and allow time for opening greetings and courtesies. Do not forget that the person who has agreed to see you will be weighing you up in those opening exchanges and considering just how much he or she will be willing to tell you.

When you are quite certain in your mind of the object of your interview, then prepare a list of the questions you want to ask. This is being efficient and businesslike. If you can gain useful answers to most of your questions, you will have achieved the object of your visit. On the other hand, do not be so rigid in your questioning that you brush aside other information that might be offered to you. Quite often the person you are talking to will open up a whole area of interest which had never occurred to you when planning the interview. This might turn out to be of far greater value than answers to your original questions.

A key-word in successful interviewing is 'courtesy'. People who agree to talk to you are doing you a favour and so you should respond to their goodwill with politeness and consideration. This would include a well-written letter or a well-spoken phone call to arrange the time and place. Punctuality should be observed in keeping the appointment. A good appearance and an agreeable manner are important.

The use of your note-book is worth a moment's thought. Some people are inhibited if they see you writing down everything they say and will talk more freely if they feel they are just conversing with you. If you are gathering facts and figures, ask if you may write them down – a request that is unlikely to be refused. Your interviewee may be someone in a public position. In this case you must be quite sure that you report him or her accurately and if you are told something 'off the record', you must respect this confidence absolutely.

Suspicion of a note-book is nothing compared to the fear some people have of a tape-recorder. If you are anxious to tape-record some of the interview, you must of course ask permission, but before you do this, ask yourself if the microphone is likely to worry your interviewee and make him or her reluctant to speak freely. The very sight of a tape-recorder or note-book will make some people nervous, so keep both hidden in your bag until you are sure that neither will be counter-productive!

Being interviewed

An interview by your teacher for GCSE assessment can take various forms. It may occur spontaneously, with your teacher engaging you in conversation and asking questions designed to draw you out on a topic the class is working on or an outside activity in which you are known to be involved. The interview might be set up in advance, with due warning given that on such-and-such a day you will be interviewed on a specified topic. If this happens, then use the time to prepare.

You may be asked to explain a project you are working on or to describe an event in which you have taken part. In such a case, plan what you want to bring out in the interview, thinking of the most important aspects of your topic and the best ways of describing them. It would be a help if you brought along visual aids – drawings, models, and other exhibits which are relevant – and these could be used during the conversation to make your points more clear. If two of you are being interviewed at the same time (as is quite possible if you are working together on a project) then decide in advance how you are going to share out the responsibility. One of you might talk about the materials needed and how you acquired them, while the other might go on to describe how they were used.

Who takes control in an interview? Is it the teacher-assessor or is it you? In fact each of you has an area of authority. The person who sets up the interview and begins by asking the leading questions is at first the dominant figure, and you would be accustomed to regarding your teacher as a figure of authority. Yet *you* are the person who holds the interesting information and whose views are being sought. You are the one who knows the subject under discussion and who holds the views that the interviewer wants to hear. Therefore, from this point of view, you are the person in authority and, once the interview begins, you may find that more and more you are leading the conversation because you are the person who knows more about the topic and your interviewer is wanting to hear you talk about it. A skilful teacher-assessor will try to encourage you to take up this position of authority so that you can talk freely and with confidence about what interests you. Be prepared to welcome this development and contribute to it. If you merely reply to leading questions with short answers and do not extend the conversational openings which you are given, you will force the interviewer to do more and more of the talking and will show yourself less than successful in one-to-one conversations.

Do not feel that you are under some sort of obligation to accept everything that is said to you in an interview. You have the right to question and even challenge remarks made by an interviewer. Sometimes things are said with the intention of seeing if you will passively accept them or whether or not you have the independence of mind to examine them critically. Of course this must be done with tact and discretion: not every employer would look favourably on an applicant who differed from him too vigorously!

As in all speech activities, an ability to *listen* is important. Be sure that you listen carefully to questions that are put to you and that you fully understand their implications. Avoid being so carried away by what you are saying that you take no notice of challenges by the interviewer. Remember that an interview is a conversation with two partners and that the interviewer may quite unexpectedly change the line of discussion. Your ability to respond rapidly to this change of situation would be noted.

Some people, when they are conversing with only one other person, seem to think that clear speech is less important than when speaking to a large group. Naturally the tone and style will be different, but a private interview is no excuse for indistinct speech and mumbled answers. Keep the tone bright and lively and make it easy for the interviewer to follow without effort everything you have to say.

Giving a Talk

You are very likely to be asked to prepare and give a talk at some time during your GCSE course. It may feature as part of an end-of-course assessment (it is compulsory for the London and East Anglian Group), or it may happen more than once during your assessed class-work. It is the most obvious example of 'talk as product', which teachers are required to include. So it is very probable that one day your teacher will say to you, 'I want you to think of a topic that interests you, plan a talk on it and be prepared to give it on such-and-such a date.'

Panic! Whatever can you talk about? Your mind goes completely blank and, when you recover, the one or two subjects that occur to you seem impossibly dull. 'No one wants to listen to me talking about that,' you tell yourself. 'I don't know anything about anything. I'm not really interested in anything at all!'

This is a common nervous reaction to the request to give a talk *and it is almost certainly completely untrue*. You *are* interested in certain things and other people will be interested to hear what you have to say. The problem is convincing yourself of this. Just remember that enthusiasm is catching. If you are really interested in a certain activity and talk about it freshly and naturally, your audience will quickly respond by close attention followed by lively questioning.

Some people would say that 'Knitting' sounds a very dull subject for a talk. But is it dull? Not if you are enthusiastic about your hobby, talk about how you gained your skill, show some articles you have made, speak of the next garment you are planning – and tell your listeners how they can start knitting if they want to! The great thing is to be interested yourself.

There is something about a GCSE talk that you should know: *it should stimulate discussion from the group when you have finished.* It may also provide a talking point for you in an interview with your teacher. The National Criteria, to which all syllabuses have to conform, says of talks: 'They . . . have a useful role to play in the assessment of the spoken language by providing useful contexts for the interview and/or discussion in which both listening and speaking are to be assessed.' You should not, therefore, expect your presentation to end when you have finished your prepared talk. It will be followed by questions and discussion on which you and your fellow students could be assessed. In practice, you will find that the discussion session will very possibly be the most enjoyable part of the experience when everyone joins in to talk about your topic and to ask more about it.

You will also be able to bring visual and aural aids to enhance your talk. How to make the best use of them will be discussed later in this chapter.

But what can I talk about?

You may by now have agreed that perhaps people may be prepared to show an interest in what you have to say, but the problem still remains: you have to choose a topic. You may have no obvious hobby and your life may seem a very ordinary round of school, homework, TV and a Saturday job. But even this may contain the seeds of a talk ('My Favourite TV Programme', 'People I Meet on Saturdays', 'Why Homework is Good for You'). Take a piece of paper and write down the answers to the questionnaire given below, and surprise yourself by discovering all the things you know about. The answers will not necessarily be topics for talks, but they will be pointers and, after you have responded, you will be shown how to use the answers to find subjects you did not know were there . . .

1. Name the city/town/village where you live.
2. Where else have you lived?
3. Have you lived or travelled abroad? Where and when?
4. What career are you hoping to follow?
5. What work do your parents do (or have done)?
6. How do you spend (a) the evenings (b) the weekends?
7. What are your hobbies?
8. What sports are you interested in? Do you take an active part in them?

9. Have you any friends or relatives with unusual jobs or hobbies?
10. What is your favourite school subject?
11. Are you interested in music? Do you play an instrument?
12. Are you interested in acting, dancing, painting, craft work, etc.?
13. Which, if any, of these general areas interest you? Outdoor activities, the environment, history, travel, animals, science and technology, books, cooking.
14. What topics of public interest do you feel strongly about?
15. What would be your ideal holiday?

As you wrote out the answers, it is possible that a good subject for a talk leapt out at you. That means you have nothing more to worry about . . . except preparing the talk and delivering it! But suppose your paper has a large number of gaps and what you have written down still looks very uninteresting and no idea for a talk suggests itself. What do you do now?

The first thing to realize is that your answers were pointers *towards* a talk, not necessarily topics in themselves. You have to think hard about your answers and see if a possible subject is there just below the surface. For example, you may have filled in No. 6 as 'Baby Sitting'. No talk there, you think. But you are wrong! What about a talk on the first (or second or third) year of a baby's life, using the baby you look after as an example? You will know a great deal about him already and you can ask his mother more details about when he began to crawl, to get his first tooth, to start to talk and so on. You can follow this up by reading about child development and you then have plenty of material for an excellent talk.

Places where you live – or have lived – are also very productive. Your personal knowledge will be the starting point but you can build it up by talking to your family and reading up in guide books, local histories and so on. The talk could be on any one of many aspects of the town – its history, its industries, its attractions, its people – or you might choose to talk of just one place in it (cathedral, theatre, leisure centre). Perhaps there is a stately home nearby, a famous beauty spot or the site of a famous battle. The more you think the more possibilities occur.

If you have lived abroad, the topic is likely to be even more interesting because it will be less familiar to your audience. You could compare family life in that country with the way of life at home; you could contrast school life with our own; you could describe the leisure pursuits possible in that country but not in ours. Some people would find interesting material in the local methods of cooking and could demonstrate how to prepare an exotic dish. Others might be able to display the clothes worn in that country and discuss local fashions and folk customs.

The jobs done by parents and friends can be very productive of ideas. There may be someone you know who does a really unusual job. You might get him or her to tell you about it and perhaps give you some reading material on it as well. This would afford you the chance to exercise your spoken English by interviewing the person (see pp. 28–30). You might even find a long-lost relative – like the boy who filled in such a questionnaire and remembered an obscure uncle who was a judge in Fiji! He obtained his address from his grandmother in Australia and wrote to the judge, who was so delighted to find a nephew he had never heard of that he sent him a large pack of material on Fiji – and a present as well! The result was a very good talk – and two happy people.

Practical activities are very good subjects for talks because they allow you to demonstrate a skill or show exhibits. Craft work of all kinds gives plenty of scope – model-making, needle-work, pottery, flower arranging, metal work, carpentry – or knitting (as previously mentioned). Not only does such a subject create interest, but the speaker often surprises fellow students who never knew he or she was so talented.

If you have responded to question 13 and written down one or more of the general topics listed there, you will have to narrow it down to a specific title. If you have selected 'History', then a historical personage, a famous place or an event in history might be your choice. 'Science' could produce all sorts of things from a description of a scientific process to thoughts on how science will transform the world in a hundred years' time. 'Animals' would suggest a wide selection of topics from 'Keeping a Pet' or 'African Safaris' to 'Animal Rights' and the pros and cons of vivisection.

Despite all this good advice, you may still be looking at your list of answers with dull despair. Even now there seems to be no talk among them. This is probably the time for a word of advice from someone who will come fresh to your list. This might be your teacher or a parent or a friend. Show the person your list and see if he or she can spot an opening that will lead to a talk you can make something of. Try not to be negative or dismissive of every suggestion. Remember that you are capable of interesting other people and that somewhere there is a topic (perhaps several topics) which will be just right for you. Remember too that you do not have to be good at *written* English in order to speak in a lively and interesting way. Many students who have considered themselves poor at English (meaning written English) have gained respect from their colleagues for their ability to *talk* well on a subject that interests them.

Topics to beware of!

An interest in a topic is a great asset, but it does not necessarily guarantee success. Interest is important but you need good material to back it up – and for some subjects it is very hard to find sufficient material. An outstanding example of this is Pop Music. Of course it interests you very much; of course you enjoy it and spend a good deal of time listening to it. But do you know enough about it to give a talk?

Candidates often choose to talk about a pop group because they like its music. But what is there to say? The names of the players, their backgrounds, their successes and their future plans – surely this is enough to make a good talk? Certainly it is if you know all this in plenty of detail. But do you? Most teenagers have remarkably little information about their favourite group beyond what they find on a record sleeve or perhaps in a magazine article. In far too many cases, the so-called talk becomes a list of names and placings in the charts and nothing else. The *music* of the pop musicians is what is interesting and entertaining. Unless you really do know a great deal about the music, the musicians, the record companies and so on, you will simply not have enough to say! While you are floundering around to spin out this topic, you will be ignoring much more interesting subjects which you know a great deal about. So think twice before you decide to talk about a pop group or a pop star.

The same applies to football teams – another quite popular choice. Really good talks are possible on the recent performances of famous teams or on their histories, but too often the talk degenerates into a list of results and of team players. It takes plenty of knowledge and skill to give vivid descriptions of famous games or to assess the abilities of certain players. What is more, you are unlikely to be able to read up very much about your team in order to increase your knowledge, unless you can research the files of the local newspaper for many seasons. As always, think of your listeners and ask yourself if you have enough information to keep them interested – even for three minutes.

What am I going to say?

Once you have decided on your topic, you face the problem of finding material for it: what are you going to say?

Begin by putting together as much information as you can. This will be the bricks from which you will construct your talk. Do not be in too much of a hurry to plan what you are going to say. Make sure first of all that you have *enough* to say.

Ask yourself

There are three principal sources of information on a chosen subject. The first is yourself. You have made the decision that you are going to speak on a certain topic and therefore you presumably know something about it. Jot down a number of things which you think you would like to tell your listeners and see what they amount to. You may have so much to say that you cover three sides of paper non-stop. This is possible but not very likely. More probably, writing that list will show you what you don't know – and there is no harm in this. If your personal material is so impossibly thin that you cannot get beyond the third line, you ought seriously to consider another subject. But assuming you have written down some useful items, you will almost certainly realize that there are gaps in your knowledge.

Perhaps your chosen subject was 'Keeping a Cat'. Your personal knowledge is based on the pet you have at home. Your jottings will have recorded how you trained it from a kitten, the kind of food it likes best and what inoculations it has had. At this point you realize that the material may not be quite enough for a talk of three minutes or longer. What is more, the listeners will want to ask questions and you cannot be sure of the answers. For example, your reference to inoculations may lead someone to ask about the illnesses a cat may suffer and so you need to find out something about that. You ought to be able to discuss what breed of cat yours is and what its characteristics are. Possibly a comparison with some other well-known breeds would be useful in your talk. Now you can see that your personal knowledge needs to be reinforced by a little research.

Ask other people

The second source of information (after yourself) is other people. Depending on the subject, much valuable material can be gained from talking to others. Your own parents may remember some useful things about the cat which you have forgotten; perhaps they have the pedigree certificate locked away somewhere. The vet may spare you five minutes to tell you about common cat diseases and the local pet shop owner may chat to you about the cats he sells and the people who buy them. If there is specific information you want people to give you, then follow the advice for conducting interviews given on pp. 28–30. A casual conversation can be useful, but a properly organized interview is more likely to be productive.

Ask the library

The third source of information is the printed word – books, magazines, leaflets, etc. It is to these that the researcher most frequently turns. But you can waste a great deal of time in a library idly turning over pages of books and still not finding what you want. Be businesslike in order to save yourself time. Decide before you go to the library exactly what you want to know and then seek advice on the best way to find it. If you have not been trained how to use a library, approach a librarian for help. Ask what you want to know and where the information can be found. This short conversation will save you long periods of frustration as you vainly search the shelves for books that do not exist, whereas a librarian could put the books you want in your hands within a matter of minutes – or else tell you frankly that no such books are available.

Encyclopedia

When you use an encyclopedia or any other large work of reference, *begin with the index*. You may find what you want under the alphabetical entries or you may not. What is certain, however, is that you are likely to find more page references in the index than in the single volume you are consulting. A well-known encyclopedia has no less than *fourteen* references in its index to 'cats', requiring the use of ten different volumes. It deals in various places with such things as cats' hair, teeth and breathing; the care of cats; superstitions about them; wild cats; the different breeds of domestic cat – and so on and so on. This is much more than you would find by just looking up 'cats' under C in a single volume!

Writing to firms

Not every subject is written about in an encyclopedia or a hard-back book. Business firms and other organizations often have information packs about their activities and these can be useful when you are researching an appropriate topic. One word of warning! It is wrong to waste the time of a big firm by writing to it for material which is already easily available in your own school library. Some firms are very generous in responding to requests for information, but others are rightly irritated by thoughtless, casual requests that cost them time and money. If you do write to a firm for such help, make sure the letter is polite and well written – and enclose a stamped addressed envelope for their reply!

The beginning

The speaker who begins 'My talk is about cats' is at least clear and straightforward. You know what you are in for. On the other hand, you may not be very excited at the prospect. The art of the speaker is to win the attention of the audience and suggest to them that they are about to hear something really interesting and possibly exciting. Just to announce the topic is a rather dull way to start. It is even worse to say 'I am going to *do* my talk on cats.' This makes it sound like an unpleasant task that has to be got through as soon as possible and everybody present is being asked to put up with it. This may be absolutely true, but your talk will be much more effective if you can choose an opening that will promise the listeners at least some interest and enjoyment along the way.

'In this basket I have a creature who is the first cousin of lions and tigers!' (You then lift the lid of the basket and Tiddles peers nervously over the edge.) This opening will have created some stir of interest and will enable you to lead in to the history of the breed, as planned.

Another useful opening is the challenging question. If your subject is 'Road Safety', you might begin, 'Do you know the killer who destroyed hundreds of children last year in this country alone? The answer is – the motor vehicle!' With this frightening statistic you have gripped the attention of your listeners.

A very short story, especially of a personal experience, often provides an excellent opening: 'Last year my family moved into an old cottage in the country. When we were clearing out the roof space beneath the thatch, we found a child's shoe. It was made of leather and obviously dated from the Middle Ages. Someone told me it was a medieval custom to place a shoe in the roof to ward off evil spirits. This made me want to know more about these old customs and this is what I would like to tell you about today.' In this way you could introduce a talk on 'Old Superstitions'.

Keep your opening short and simple, but use your imagination to find ways of alerting your audience to the fact that you are about to interest them – not put them to sleep.

The middle

One of the elements of oral English that your assessors will be taking note of is your ability to order and structure what you have to say. This is no more unusual than expecting a piece of written work to have a beginning, a middle and an end. Yet it has to be thought about, for a talk will not fall into place by chance.

Let's assume that by now your topic has been chosen and the material for it gathered together from your own experience, your personal inquiries and your research. Next you have to select the material you need and shape it into a satisfying presentation.

Within the context of an assessment your talk is likely to be around three to four minutes long. This does not seem a very long time but it is surprising how much can be said within this space. It is quite adequate for an interesting exploration of a process or a point of view, a personal memory or an activity. On the other hand, it is quite easy (for some people, at any rate) to ramble on for very much longer if you have not carefully worked out in advance what can and cannot be said within that time-limit. The really off-putting thing would be for the assessor to interrupt you because you were going well beyond the time available. This makes you look foolish and perhaps lose the best point you were saving up for a climax. Timing is therefore essential.

Choose three or four main points that you wish to make. If we continue with our example of 'Cats', you may decide to talk about care of the animal, including veterinary treatment and illnesses to guard against, the cat's early days and training, the breed and its general characteristics, its feeding habits and daily routine. Each of these would give you a main section to your talk, but you have to decide the best order in which to present these points. It might be best to start with some general remarks about the breed, introduce your own cat (in person or in pictures), talk of its early days and how you trained it, then go on to present its daily routine and conclude with remarks on its health care. Such a talk would have order and shape.

The end

Too many talks just stop dead. The audience are suddenly aware that there is a horrid silence: the speaker looks embarrassed and the listeners feel awkward. One moment they are following with interest and the next moment there is silence. Be sure this does not happen when you are giving a talk. It could ruin the effect of an otherwise very good presentation. You can easily avoid this fault by giving just a few minutes' thought about the way you bring your talk to an end.

In a talk lasting only three minutes or so you have no time for a lengthy conclusion. All that is needed is a neat remark that clearly signals to the audience that the talk has ended. It is best if this follows quite naturally from your final point. Perhaps you have been describing how to look after a pony. Having gone through the whole process, you might finish with the remark, 'And that is how you groom a pony' or 'If you follow this routine, your pony will be as happy and healthy as mine is.' These endings are brief and to the point, but they obviously indicate that you have finished what you want to say.

Another possible ending, which can be used with almost any subject, is to remark, 'I hope I have said something to interest you in . . . (naming the topic).' This formula can be varied and improved in all sorts of ways, but however you adapt it, you will be able to finish the talk with some style. Certainly it will be better than saying pathetically (after an awful pause), 'Please, I've finished!'

Stand and deliver

It is a good idea to stand up when you give your talk. Of course it is possible to give a good talk sitting down and you may be allowed to do so during an assessment. Yet giving a talk is a formal speech activity and should be treated as such. (There are plenty of less formal speech activities during an English course.) A formal activity suggests that you are doing something special and your appearance, stance, choice of words and manner should reflect this. Whether you like it or not, you are on show.

Another advantage of standing is that you can make use of visual aids more easily than if you are sitting. This is particularly true of drawings and diagrams pinned to a wall or board behind you, but it would also apply to hand-held exhibits, which are much easier to see if you are on your feet.

Can I read the talk?

YOU MUST NOT READ YOUR TALK.

There can be no question about this. An essay is an essay and a talk is a talk. The first is meant to be read silently and the second is meant to be spoken aloud. The kind of language you use will differ from one to the other. You should not confuse the two. In any case, your teacher-assessor will not allow you to write out a speech and then read it aloud.

People work in different ways when they are preparing a talk. Some will write down a bare outline, being confident that they can provide the details spontaneously when they begin to speak. Others (especially beginners) will feel they must write down every word. If you share this feeling, then try to hear yourself *saying* the words as you write them – that is, think of them all the time as *spoken English* and not as the English you would write in a composition. This means that shortened forms (it's, can't, haven't, aren't, etc.) and conversational phrases will be included, whereas they would be inappropriate in an essay.

Once you have written out the talk and satisfied yourself about its shape and contents, go through it and underline the main points. Read the talk through a number of times (not too often, by the way), concentrating on these main points and then see how much you can say without looking at the script. You should not try to memorize the whole speech – *only the main points.* The additional material will already be in your mind but will come over much more effectively if you express yourself freshly rather than try painfully to remember the precise wording you had used in your script. When you stand up to speak, you will not be without support: if you wish to do so, you may use notes.

Notes

The person who can talk directly to the audience without any piece of paper in hand or on the desk is much to be admired. But most of us feel happier with at least something to remind us what to say next. Of course the less you use your notes the better, because they are bound to be something of a barrier – even a very small one – between you and the audience. Therefore put only the minimum of information on to your notes, so that the temptation to read aloud rather than to speak directly is removed as far as possible. Too often one finds that a candidate's note-cards are not notes but the whole speech written in very small handwriting. This achieves the worst of all worlds: the speech is read and not spoken and the handwriting is so small that the speaker has to peer at it closely in order to read it at all!

The most convenient form of notes is a set of cards – about postcard size. Number them and write not more than two or three main points on each. Be sure you write very clearly, possibly in block capitals. It is essential that you can read your own notes quickly and easily. As you use them, move each card in turn to the bottom of the pack, quietly and unobtrusively. Avoid flexing them, waving them about – or dropping them. The cards are your silent friends, giving you a gentle reminder of what to say next. Do not let them become a distraction.

Visual aids

Talks are all the better for something to look at apart from you. Most topics can have a visual element – pictures, diagrams, maps and exhibits of all kinds. They not only create interest among your listeners; they actively assist you in your talk. Think of how difficult it would be to describe adequately how to cook a complicated dish, and how much easier it would be if all the ingredients were displayed on the table and the dish itself in various stages of preparation. It is also much easier to follow the story of a journey if the speaker uses a map rather than relying entirely on his own words. A well-drawn chart will bring dull statistics to life very quickly. Here are some hints about using visual aids:

1. Make sure your visual aids are big enough to be seen by all the audience. (A small snapshot is rarely of much use.)
2. Avoid the error of passing exhibits around the audience while you are speaking. This loses the attention of each listener in turn, just when you want everyone to be concentrating on you.
3. Consider using another person as a visual aid! This can be very useful if you are demonstrating a practical skill such as first aid, dancing or fencing – or if you are describing a fashion.
4. But think twice before using an animal as a visual aid. This *can* be very successful, providing the pet is docile. But you run the risk of the animal wrecking the presentation by moving about or even misbehaving itself. If you decide it is worth the risk, then bring a friend who will take charge of the animal when you are not actually demonstrating it. The hamster back in his box or the dog outside the door will enable you to go on with your talk without further worries – and as for snakes . . .
5. If you show slides to illustrate your talk, make sure before you begin that the equipment is in good working order.
6. Avoid talking at length over the whirring of a noisy projector.
7. It is usually better to show a very few well-chosen slides; otherwise your talk becomes a slide show.
8. Before you decide to use slides, consider the possible disruption that may be caused if you need a black-out during all or part of your talk.
9. Slide illustrations can be excellent, but think carefully how, why and when it will be to your advantage to use them.

Aural aids

The most common form of aural aid is a tape-recording. You might also give a 'live' demonstration of a musical instrument you have been talking about. Nowadays visual aids and aural aids can be combined in a video. All these are useful, providing they do not take over your talk. The audience – and the assessor – want to hear what you have to say. You will be penalized if you speak only briefly, filling up the time with long recorded extracts.

Talks of All Kinds . . .

Up to now the advice on presenting a talk has been based on the assumption that you have had a free choice of topic and have opted to speak about a hobby or interest of your own. But this is not the only form that a GCSE talk can take. Here is a short list of suggestions for other kinds of talks, gathered from the suggestions in the syllabuses of the Examining Boards: presenting a point of view, taking part in a debate, narrating a story, giving instructions, introducing a discussion topic and reporting back on a discussion. This last item has already been considered in the chapter on 'Discussion' (pp. 26–7).

Much of what has been said already about planning and presenting your talk would apply in these situations also, but we will look at these in turn to see the particular problems and opportunities that each has to offer.

Presenting a point of view

You may have the chance to give your talk on one of the many issues about which people these days feel strongly . . . such things as the treatment of children and the elderly, nuclear policy, animal rights, the destruction of the countryside, urban development policy and so on. All the advice given in the preceding sections still applies: the need for researching your subject; careful planning; a good beginning and a good ending. Here are some additional hints that apply especially to this kind of topic:

1. Be sure you know what you are talking about! It is very easy to become emotional over some burning issue of the day and you may be tempted to choose a topic because it has been on TV or in

the newspapers recently. There is no harm in this – on the contrary, it could be a good topical choice – providing you have done your homework on the subject. If you choose to talk about it to a group, you are exposing yourself to questions from your audience and perhaps their contrary opinions. You therefore have to know the subject very well indeed so that you can stand up as an authority on the problem, answering questions adequately and replying to those with opposite views. You do not want to be shown up as someone ignorant of important aspects of the very subject you have chosen to talk about!

2. There are two sides to most questions. However eager you are to press your point of view, you will be more effective if you treat the other side of the argument fairly and honestly, even while you are trying to demolish it.
3. Give specific examples to illustrate the points you are making. A long theoretical discussion, all facts and figures, can quickly become boring. Bring it to life with vivid illustrations of the point you are arguing. If an example has your own personal experience behind it, you will be even more successful. Just imagine the difference in effect between a speaker who reels off nothing but statistics on road accidents and another speaker who begins, 'When I was knocked down by a car . . .!'
4. Do not try to say too much. Two or three clear-cut and telling points will be remembered by the audience when seven or eight small points all muddled together will be forgotten quickly. Choose a strong opening argument to catch the sympathy of your audience and save up a really clinching point to serve as your conclusion.

Debating

Another form which your talk might take is a speech in a debate. This is a highly formal activity, governed by firm rules of the game. These can be as elaborate as those in Parliament or as uncomplicated as your class cares to make them. Essentially a debate is a contest in which speakers argue on one side of a case or the other with the aim of persuading their listeners to support their cause at the end of the session. A debate always ends in a vote with one side or the other being declared the winner. The issue being discussed is known as the motion and the body of people considering it is referred to as 'this House'. Therefore the motion usually begins with the words, 'In the opinion of this House . . .' Then follow the details of what is being proposed. An example would be: 'In the opinion of this House, homework should be abolished.'

The first speaker is the Proposer and he or she rises to put the case for abolishing homework. Then follows the Opposer, who makes a speech giving the opposite view. Next come two more principal speakers, the Seconders of each side. If you wish, you can have three, four or even more supporting principal speakers. These would be expected to have prepared their speeches in advance; but when the principal speakers have finished, the debate is said to be 'open to the floor of the House'. This means that anyone present may rise and make a short speech, usually impromptu, for or against the motion.

The whole proceedings are controlled by the chairman. All remarks are addressed to the Chair and not to other members of the House. This is to prevent angry exchanges between individuals. Depending on the rules you adopt, it will probably not be permissible to interrupt speakers, except under certain agreed circumstances. It is best to let each speaker have his or her say and then members reply to controversial points in subsequent speeches. Members indicate their wish to speak by raising a hand or standing up and the chairman calls the speaker by name, others giving way until that speech is finished. Towards the end of the debate, the Proposer is allowed to 'wind up' with a last appeal for support. Then the chairman reads the motion again, takes the vote and declares the motion either to be carried or defeated.

A speech for a debate has some similarities with a talk on a topical issue, already discussed. But the principal aim of a debating speech is to persuade people to adopt your point of view. You must be purposely one-sided! You should show little sympathy for any argument of your opponents (except to show that such sympathy is far outweighed by the pressure of your own arguments).

You and your Seconders should get together and write down all the points you can think of in favour of your case. Add to this as many striking examples and illustrations as you can. From this list decide how you are going to share out the arguments. Obviously the Proposer and Opposer will need some impressive points to launch the case, but you should leave something fresh and effective for the speeches of the Seconders. If the subject is wide enough, you may be able to allocate the most important area to the Proposer (or Opposer) and a completely different aspect of the case to a Seconder.

Consider too the likely arguments of the opposition. Forewarned is forearmed! Every speaker from the Opposer onwards will have a chance of replying to arguments of a previous speaker. Only the Proposer, who opens the debate, is not in this position until the end; that is why he is given the privilege of the final speech. You have to decide very quickly if you are going to tackle the arguments already put forward. You may prefer to ignore them altogether and deliver your own prepared speech as it stands. However, much of the fun of a debate comes from the impromptu responses to previous points and a debate in which the speakers stuck rigidly to their prepared notes would be a very dull affair. It is usually the Seconders who have the most enjoyment shooting down the arguments of the previous speakers, but members talking from the 'floor' in open debate can also join in.

If you are asked to be the chairman, then establish and maintain a firm control of what is going on. You are expected to be an expert on the rules and must see that people obey them. Above all, do not let a debate become a discussion group, with everyone speaking just when he or she feels like it. Members are expected to make speeches – not short observations – and all remarks must be addressed to you, as chairman. Your class or society might make it a rule that no one is allowed to speak more than once, unless the debate has 'died' before the allocated time. A good chairman will ensure that all members have an equal chance to be heard and this control, far from inhibiting discussion, will make the proceedings go with a swing.

Telling a story

A speech activity closely allied to giving a formal talk is 'telling a story'. This sounds an easier task: your material is ready to hand in the narrative itself, visual aids will not be needed and your audience should quickly become interested in knowing 'what happened next'. But being a good story-teller is not as simple as it sounds. Some people are naturally good at it – every young child knows the member of the family who tells the best stories. But you can improve your own performance with practice.

In a GCSE class telling a story will not appear to you as natural as joining in a discussion or giving a talk on your hobby. It may arise from a Literature assignment: for example, 'Read Chapter 5 of your novel for homework and be prepared to tell the class what happens in it' or 'Summarize for the class the events of Act 3 of the play we are studying.' This becomes a kind of revision exercise and your listeners know what you are going to say anyway. The activity becomes more real if you have the chance to offer a plot of your own choice and would be even more real if you were able to visit a junior school and tell a story to the children there. However, your story-telling is likely to be an assignment within your own classroom.

If you are asked to prepare a story to tell to a group of fellow students, you first need to know if you are expected to compose an original story or if you may choose a tale you have heard or read elsewhere. Writing your own short story is a challenging business and beyond the scope of this book to discuss, but whether you use your own plot or are telling someone else's, there are some points worth bearing in mind when you become a 'teller of tales'.

1. Keep the story-line simple. Some of the most famous short stories in the world are the parables of Jesus – The Good Samaritan, The Prodigal Son, etc. Notice how each story is uncluttered by extraneous details and how clear and easy each is to follow, with just one main event and everything directed towards the climax. It is best therefore to avoid the temptation to re-tell the plot of a long novel or the adventures of a hero in a television series. These pack in very many incidents and twists and turns of plot to keep their audiences entertained, but they are very difficult to summarize in a five-minute story-telling session. If you attempt this, you will quickly find yourself bogged down with unmanageable complications.
2. Concentrate on one central character only – for reasons similar to

those given above. A central character with no more than two or three others who have dealings with him are manageable, but a large cast of characters will tax the memories and concentration of both you and your audience.

3. Keep the descriptions to a necessary minimum for scene-setting and the creation of atmosphere. Your listeners will want to know what happened and so do not delay them by lengthy descriptions and background explanations.
4. Decide what is to be the climax of your story. Work towards this and when you have achieved it, bring the story to an end with as little subsequent explanation as is necessary to round off the tale.
5. Be clear and direct in your opening. The tellers of old folk tales knew their business: 'Once upon a time there was a poor fisherman who had two sons. One day the younger caught a fish and, on cutting it open, found inside it a golden ring . . .'

   Consider what we have gained from those two sentences: we have been introduced to three principal characters; we know that they are fishermen and that they are poor; we have also been told the surprising discovery from which the whole story will develop. All this in under thirty words! Already the listeners will be intrigued and anxious to know what the young man did with the ring.
6. Present the right points in the right order. This means careful planning in advance. Just because you know the plot, do not assume that preparing an outline is unnecessary. The planning stage is very similar to that for a talk with the preparation of notes and rehearsing the final presentation, as already described.
7. Speak clearly! The effect of your well-prepared story will be lost if your speech is indistinct. Projecting a story is more than a matter of voice. The good story-teller re-lives the tale he is telling and this is reflected in his facial expressions and even his stance. These should not be 'put on' because that will look false and artificial. Have confidence in your story and allow your voice and facial expression to reflect quite naturally the movement of the narrative.

Giving instructions

'Giving instructions about what?' you may ask. The answer is 'About anything within your experience on which you can instruct others.' A short impromptu exercise might be to tell a stranger how to walk from the railway station to your school. At the other end of the scale, you might be asked to give a talk instructing the whole class on the best way to set up a tropical fish tank or how to strip down the engine of a motor-cycle.

It should go without saying that to instruct other people you have to know what you are talking about. Make sure therefore that you really are clear in your own mind about your topic. If you have only a hazy idea of how to bake a cake, you are not likely to be very successful as a cookery instructor.

The best advice is to put yourself in your listeners' place. Think how much or how little they know about your topic. It is very easy to assume that your listeners know more than they do. This is particularly true of technical terms. To tell a group of absolute beginners in a dance class to 'plié' would be meaningless to them, whereas 'bend your knees' would be immediately acted upon. Using technical words is often a form of showing off. When giving instructions to people who do not possess some knowledge of your subject, use the plainest layman's language and if you judge that technical terms will save time in the long run, then explain them as you go along.

Arrange the stages of your instructions in a clear, logical order, taking the listeners step by step through the process. Avoid putting yourself in the situation of having to go back to say something more about the second step in order to make sense of the fifth step. The sentence which begins, 'By the way, I should have told you that . . .' is evidence of careless planning and a poor instructor.

Visual aids are a great help when giving instructions. How to get from A to B is much easier to explain with the aid of a map. It is far simpler to show someone how to mend a puncture if you have a tyre in your hands and the repair kit beside you than trying to do the instruction entirely by word of mouth. Decide in the planning stage just how and when you are going to use the visual aids. Some speakers have been known to bring along equipment, set it up and then practically ignore it during their talk. If you have good visual aids, make them an important feature of your presentation.

It is a good idea to assume at first that people will be slower on the uptake than you might imagine, especially if the subject is quite new to them. Help them to understand each stage of what you are explaining by asking if they want you to repeat what you have said or explain it further. You will quickly gather whether you are dealing with an alert group with whom you can move swiftly or with one that will make progress slowly and will need fuller explanation and demonstration from you.

At the end of your instructions, 'recap' briefly on what you have explained and then ask for any questions.

Introducing a discussion topic

Taking part in a discussion involves a different kind of speaking from the more formal style you would use when giving a talk. But if you are asked to *introduce* a topic to a group which has to discuss it, you are in fact being called on to make a speech. You may be sitting in a circle with the group or around the same table, but your remarks are going to be of a different kind from those which follow in the discussion. What you are going to deliver – although it may only last a couple of minutes – is a formal speech and the advice given earlier will still apply: preparation, planning, possibly the use of notes and good clear speech.

Once you have been given the topic – or have made your own choice – you have to be quite sure you fully understand the subject yourself. It is no good inviting people to talk about poverty in the Third World if you have only a vague idea of what the Third World is! Your job is to announce the topic clearly, explain what it involves and suggest certain aspects which the group may care to explore.

A good way of gaining interest and attention is to read a short paragraph on the subject from a recent newspaper or magazine. This will emphasize that the topic concerns people here and now. A newspaper report is likely to contain graphic details of the subject and could well suggest talking points too. A very short story, in your own words, that shows how the discussion topic affects people is another excellent way of bringing it to life for the group and stimulating talk.

Having read the newspaper cutting or related the story, announce clearly what the subject of the discussion arising from your introduction is to be. (Do not assume that the group will deduce this for itself.) You then have to move with care: you want to suggest possible areas of discussion, but you should avoid saying so much that the group feel there is nothing left to discuss. In preparing the introduction, think of three or four major talking points. You do not have to make up your own mind about them: your own views may develop, like everyone else's, during the discussion. The points should be controversial of course; otherwise there will be nothing to discuss. Place them before the group but leave the members to find their own way into them. They are under no compulsion to discuss the points in the order you mentioned them: they may even prefer to bring up and discuss points of their own. Having introduced the subject, you have to step back and let the group take over, becoming an ordinary member of the group yourself, unless you have been specifically asked to act as chairman. In this case, your role is different and has already been discussed (pp. 24–6).

Reading Aloud

Reading aloud may not, at first sight, seem a very important speech activity or one you would often indulge in when you leave school. You could be wrong! What about reading stories to your own children one day? Although a little remote from the concerns of a GCSE course, it is a reality that should eventually face all parents. Very young children learn language from their parents – fathers as well as mothers – but they will not learn adequately unless they are talked to freely and often. Next in importance to frequent talk is the reading aloud of stories. A parent who can read well and enjoys doing so brings enormous pleasure to the child: but, even more important, he or she also builds up the child's store of language. Learning to read well could be one of the most important skills you acquire.

In the adult world, there are many other opportunities to read aloud, and the ability to do it well will stand you in good stead. People working in offices often have to read messages over the phone and read back letters and reports to check the typing. In the business world reports and other documents have to be read aloud to colleagues, and in social organizations secretaries are called on to read the minutes of previous meetings and treasurers their financial reports. There is also a valuable service to be given to the elderly, the handicapped and the sick in reading aloud to them. It is far from true to say that reading aloud is an unimportant speech activity.

The GCSE Examination recognizes that reading aloud has a place in oral English work and most Examination Groups list it in their syllabuses as an activity that may be assessed. Coupled with this, there is often the requirement that you, as reader, should introduce the passage you are going to present.

Introducing a reading

The introduction to a reading passage should not be lengthy. Begin with a sentence announcing the title of the book and its author. Make sure these can be heard clearly. Book titles are often unusual and unexpected, because they are designed to intrigue the potential reader; be sure to announce the title distinctly so that even if the audience does not immediately understand its significance, at least they are in no doubt as to what it is. An author's name may not be as well known as, say, Charles Dickens or Agatha Christie. Therefore make sure the audience can register this too without difficulty. You must know from your own experience as a listener how often a reader will 'throw away' the title of a book and the name of its author – and how irritating this is.

The next thing the audience wants to know is the *kind* of book you have chosen. Is it a modern novel, a classic, a piece of science fiction, a romance, a travel book, a biography, a thriller . . . or what? Let them know this straight away and this will lead on to a short statement about the book itself. Resist the temptation to tell the plot in detail, attempting to condense the whole of 300 pages into a 30-second summary. If the author needed all those words to tell his story, how can you compete in a brief introduction? What you can do, however, is indicate in a few sentences the main theme of the book. For example, if you were introducing an historical novel, you might say, 'This book tells the story of a boy whose family is caught up in the Civil War in seventeenth-century England. His father is a staunch cavalier but his elder brother is a secret sympathizer with the Roundheads. The boy suspects that his brother is a spy and the book is the story of his adventures in finding out the truth: there is a very unexpected ending.' You will notice that no details are given, no elaborate twists and turns of the plot – just a very broad outline to allow the audience to adjust mentally to the kind of reading you are going to present to them.

You may be expected at this point to say why you have chosen the book and to give your personal opinion of it. You should find something more to say than just 'I chose this book because I enjoyed reading it.' Ask yourself three good reasons why somebody else might enjoy the book. It could be the gripping plot, the atmosphere of mystery or excitement, or perhaps it was the series of adventures which made you unable to put down the book until you had finished it. Ask yourself about the characters: were you able to relate to any one of them; did any of them have experiences that meant something special to you; did their story leave you with a satisfying feeling that you had lived through a worthwhile experience with them; were they vividly drawn; was the dialogue convincing, amusing, compelling? Answers to questions such as these will enable you to give convincing reasons why you chose to read from this particular book.

You conclude the introduction with brief remarks to place the passage you are going to read. You should not attempt an elaborate re-telling of what immediately precedes your extract. Just sketch in the background sufficiently to enable the passage to make sense and for the audience to understand who the principal characters in the extract are. In introducing a reading from our imaginary historical novel, it would be sufficient to say, 'The passage I am going to read occurs when the boy, whose name is Giles, has been captured by a Roundhead patrol, led by Captain Stanbury. The captain suspects that Giles is carrying a message to the Royalists in the neighbouring town. This is not true, but – as you will hear – Giles does have a secret of his own . . .'

The point of it all

Why read aloud? The answer to this question is *to communicate*. You will only be a successful reader if you keep in mind the fact that you have the printed page and the audience doesn't. They can share it only if you communicate it to them. All sorts of obstacles can stand in the way of this communication – extraneous noise, inattention on the audience's part, a boring text, even a stuffy or chilly room. But the chief obstacle is most likely to be *you*.

An audience does not demand much from a reader. The chief responsibility lies with the author of the book: it is his or her words that the audience is listening to. All that is required of the reader is that the audience is allowed to hear those words without effort, grouped together to make sense in the natural rhythms of the English language and spoken slowly enough to be taken in and understood. It does not sound much to ask, does it? Yet this kind of communication comes naturally to only a minority of people: most of us are all the better for some advice and plenty of practice. The practice is up to you, but here are some hints to improve your skill in reading aloud.

Stance

Hold your book up! If you put it on a table or hold it down too low, you will force your head to bend forward, with your chin tucked into your chest and your eyes withdrawn from your audience. A good position for the book is at chest level and held a little away from the body, so that it is easy to read from but does not obscure your face. If you are reading to a group of any size, then you should stand up to read. If you are reading in a sitting position, make sure you are not slouched in your chair. Your physical appearance and stance are part of the communication: if you look sloppy, you will probably sound sloppy.

Eye contact

It may sound strange, but quite a large amount of your communication as a reader comes not from your voice but from your eyes! If you read a passage without ever raising your eyes to your audience, you might as well be a disembodied voice: there is no lively contact between you and the listeners. As soon as you raise your eyes to them, a link is established which puts you in command of their attention and interest. They are no longer just listening to words: they are in touch with another personality who is sharing an experience with them.

Of course raising your eyes can be nerve-racking. It feels much safer to concentrate on the page and avoid that personal contact with the audience. But once you dare to look up, you will find it easier the next time and soon you will realize that, by doing this, you really are reading to people and not just to yourself.

Reading ahead

The art of knowing how to look up at your listeners depends on the skill of reading ahead – which is necessary for fluent reading anyway. Before you begin to speak, silently read the first half line and memorize it. Then, when you speak aloud, your eyes can be reading the second half of the line, and when you speak this, you will have moved ahead to register what is in the next line. In this way you always know what is coming well before you speak it and can prepare the right tone and phrasing for it. We all know how painful it is to listen to a reader who only goes from word to word.

If you read ahead in this way, you will of course see the next full stop approaching. You can raise your eyes and say that half-line from memory – that is, without looking down at the book at all! This sounds easy enough, but terror strikes with the thought that the next sentence is there waiting to be spoken and you do not know what it is. Have the courage not to look down until you have reached the full stop and then – only then – read and swiftly memorize the first few words of the next sentence and begin to speak once more. You may think this will cause a dreadfully long pause at each full stop. Such is not the case. Try it a few times with a paragraph on this page and you will find that once you have gained the technique, the pause is very brief. It brings a bonus with it – control of pace!

Pace

That short pause at each full stop will help to prevent the headlong rush that so many readers inflict on their listeners. One of the most common faults of inexperienced readers is just this: they read too fast. It is a nervous reaction to having to read aloud. A desire to get the unwelcome task over as soon as possible sends the reader scurrying down the page to the safe haven of the final full stop. It is a false security. The listeners are bored and dissatisfied and you, the reader, have denied yourself the satisfaction of sharing with them something worth hearing. Nor will you have gained much credit from an assessor.

How can you train yourself to slow down if you are a fast reader? First of all, think of your audience. They do not know the passage as you do. It is your job to communicate it to them. Think of them as you read and allow them time to take in what you are saying. When you have chosen a pace that seems suitable, remember it may still be faster than the audience would like!

Use the punctuation! It is amazing how many readers sweep over the commas and even the full stops as if they did not exist. These marks are put on the page to assist the reader to group the words into units of meaning and this involves separating one such group from another. If you ignore the punctuation, you will destroy the meaning and deprive yourself of valuable places for pause and a steadying of the pace.

Some readers start with the best intentions of adopting a good controlled pace but become faster and faster as the passage goes on. One way to counteract this is to make a fresh start with every new paragraph, checking back the rapid pace and returning to the original speed.

Of course it is possible to read far too slowly, to move at a snail's pace from phrase to phrase so that boredom rapidly descends on all present. There is no virtue in being slow for slowness's sake. A controlled pace is not necessarily a slow one. What you should aim for is a natural easy pace that resists the temptation to hurry and which enables your audience to enjoy the passage without a sense of being rushed.

Nor should the pace of the reading remain uniform throughout. Look for places where you might deliberately slow the pace for dramatic effect, and for other places where you would read more rapidly to build up the excitement. This brings to your reading that most desirable quality – variety!

Variety

Pitch, pause and intonation are three other aspects of reading aloud that will enable you to create the variety that makes for an effective presentation. The *pitch* of the human voice is capable of considerable variation, yet most of us operate within a very restricted range of notes, especially when reading aloud. (You use a much wider range when you cheer on a team or argue with your sister!) You can test your range by going to a room where nobody else can hear you (and embarrass you by asking what in the world you are up to) and speak a sentence in as deep a voice as you can – for instance, 'I can sound as low as this.' Then raise the pitch of your voice to a medium level and say 'I am speaking clear to hear.' Finally go to the top of your range, where it is almost a squeak and say 'I'm speaking very high indeed!!' This will show you what a considerable pitch range you have at your disposal – and this is available to you when you read. Of course you will rarely need the extremes of your range, but there is plenty of room for variety within the middle part of your voice. The poor reader will start on a very low note indeed and grumble along at this level, sounding dull and uninteresting – and, if possible, going lower and lower. This can happen because it is natural for the tune of a statement in English to fall to a low note at the end. The poor reader will start the next sentence where the previous one finished and will quickly reach rock bottom. Therefore adopt a pitch in the middle of the voice, a little higher than you think is normal. If you know you have a tendency to drift lower and lower, then re-establish the original pitch level when you begin a new paragraph. A really skilled reader will consciously choose different pitch levels for special effects: a low tone for a mysterious passage, a higher one for something lively and exciting. This kind of variation is particularly useful in bringing dialogue to life. The technique for this is discussed a little later on.

The pause is a very useful device for giving emphasis and achieving a dramatic effect. The listeners quickly become accustomed to your basic pace and are content to hear it flowing along. If it is suddenly interrupted by a pause, you achieve the effect of surprise and draw attention to what you have said or are about to say. Here is an example: try saying this sentence without any pause in it – 'He opened the box and inside found a dead mouse.' Then say it again with a definite pause after 'found': 'He opened the box and inside found . . . a dead mouse.' Immediately the factual statement about a dead mouse in a box becomes dramatic and surprising. Do not overdo the use of this effect: save it up for special occasions.

Intonation refers to the tunes of the voice; that is the musical patterns natural to the language which play an important part in conveying meaning. They are highly complex and we use them all the time in our natural speech. When reading aloud, try to avoid flattening out these tunes or reducing their variety and interest. On the contrary, give full play to the natural and flexible tunes of English speech so that the listeners feel that they are being spoken to in a real language and not in a limited or artificial 'reading voice'.

Dialogue

If you are reading aloud from a novel, the chances are that you will encounter dialogue – that is, conversation between characters. This is a wonderful opportunity for a good reader. Within the framework of the story-telling the reader has to act the words of the characters. The natural expression the character would use has to be conveyed to the listeners. Just for that moment, imagine how the character would speak the words in real life and try to convey that in your voice. It is a great help if you can adopt a different *pitch* for each character. For example, you might choose a low pitch for an old man and a higher one for the girl to whom he is speaking. Adopt different paces too: a child's words might go more rapidly than the adult's he is talking to. You might be able to adopt an accent appropriate to the character and certainly you should put into the words the emotion that lies behind them. A piece of dialogue that sounds no different from the narrative and descriptive material around it is a lost opportunity.

Preparing a passage

It should be clear by now that reading aloud is not an easy option. Unless you are challenged to read a passage at sight (a worthwhile but difficult skill to acquire) you should prepare your reading with care. There is no reason why you should not mark the text with signs to remind you how you intend to read. It often makes a great difference to the expressiveness of a reading if you underline in pencil the words in a sentence which will bear special emphasis. If a sentence is long and there is no punctuation within it to help you, then put in a sign, such as an arrow-head, to show you where you could take a breath. Insert a line between words where you wish to make a dramatic pause. You will not want to cover the text with pencil markings, but a few key ones here and there can be a great help.

Here is a passage specially designed for your practice. It contains dialogue and opportunities for variety of pace, pitch, emphasis and pause. When you have prepared and practised it, find a friend who will listen to you and make some helpful comments. Alternatively, you could tape-record it and subject yourself to your own severe criticism! Then re-record it, making the improvements you have found to be necessary.

. . . The old man gripped the arms of his chair and stared at the door. He had heard the outer door open and shut quietly and, after a moment, the tell-tale creaking of the stairs. Then came the sound of footsteps, light and delicate, as the visitor – surely a woman – crossed the landing and ascended his private staircase. He leant forward and his pale eyes gleamed. At last they were sending a messenger to him; at last they were prepared to negotiate. In a few seconds he would know either that his triumph was complete or that he was lost for ever.

The footsteps stopped. There was a moment during which all time stood still and then the door slowly opened.

He gave a sharp cry, made as if to rise from his chair and then fell back, panting for air, his face drawn and ghastly.

'Emma,' he cried, 'they've sent Emma back to me!'

The girl in the doorway watched him without emotion.

'Don't be foolish, grandfather,' she said in her cold voice. 'You know Emma died in the car crash three years ago. There is no need to play your tricks with me.'

'No tricks, no tricks, my dear,' he moaned. 'It was only that, just for a moment, I thought . . . I thought . . .'

His voice trailed away as he struggled to come to terms with the fact of the girl in the room and the memory of what might have been.

He made a convulsive effort and pulled himself upright.

'I was not expecting you, my dear,' he began again. 'They said they would send a messenger – someone with power to negotiate . . .'

Then he knew what she was going to say, and when she had said it, all would be lost.

'I am the one they have sent,' she said.

Poetry

Reading poetry aloud is an activity that may arise – indeed *should* arise – in an English classroom. It happens quite naturally if a group discussion of a poem in the Literature syllabus is about to take place. The obvious thing to do as a first step is to listen to the poem being read aloud: from this you will learn far more than from a silent reading. One GCSE Examination Group specifically mentions the possibility of poetry reading in its oral syllabus and it would surely be an acceptable and desirable activity in any oral English course. Some students find it personally enjoyable and many more would do so if they took the opportunity to try.

You may have to overcome some psychological barriers at first. There is the feeling that poetry is rather special (which it is) and that it therefore demands a special 'poetry voice' (which it does not). You may feel that because some poems deal with very deep human emotions they are better read silently because you would be embarrassed to voice them. The mentally lazy dismiss poetry with 'I don't understand it' and refuse to make the effort necessary to prepare a reading. All these attitudes are understandable but they may deprive you of an activity that can be very rewarding.

Rid your mind of the idea that poetry requires a 'poetry voice' – an artificial style of delivery. Verse is a heightened form of speech, no doubt; but it is also a natural expression of human emotion and experience. (It was Keats who said, 'If poetry comes not as naturally as the leaves to a tree, it had better not come at all.') You should therefore speak it naturally and sincerely in your own voice with no straining after special elocutionary effects. The advice already given on reading aloud still applies, especially the need for preparation and rehearsal, and for the control of pace, pitch, intonation and so on. But once you have accepted that naturalness is what is wanted and that your voice is quite adequate for it, there are some further points to help you make your poetry reading as effective as possible.

Choosing your poem To read a poem well you must like it, understand it, be prepared to share it – and be confident it suits your voice. It goes without saying that if you do not enjoy the poem yourself you are unlikely to make others enjoy it. There are so many poems in the

English language to choose from that there is no reason to select a poem for reading which you dislike.

The need to understand the poem is also obvious; but poems are mysterious things. The essence of poetry is to say what cannot be expressed in any other way. While it is necessary to know what the poet is getting at, you need not worry if there are a few areas where the meaning remains obscure even after several readings. Often the act of speaking a poem aloud throws light on those lines which were at first unclear.

Reading a poem aloud implies a desire to share it with others. If you do not really want to communicate the poet's words, then it is pointless to force yourself to read aloud. The result will be unfair to the poet and the poem.

You also have to recognize your limitations: you may enjoy a particular poem very much indeed, understand it completely and be anxious to share it with other people, and yet still be ill-advised to speak it aloud. Why? Because, however much you want to speak it, that poem would not suit your voice and personality. Girls have thrilled to the old heroics of Tennyson's 'The Charge of the Light Brigade' with its galloping rhythm:

> Half a league, half a league,
> Half a league onward,
> All in the valley of Death
> Rode the six hundred . . .

But the light quality of a young girl's voice is unlikely to suit this poem of thundering hooves. Nor would the deep tones of a sixteen-year-old boy easily adapt to a delicate lyric by, say, Christina Rossetti. Ask yourself if you have at present the vocal quality that will match the mood and style of the poem you are considering.

Imagination Good verse-speaking is not a mechanical act of transferring written symbols into sound. It is an act of imagination, through which the speaker shares the poet's feelings and experiences and conveys them to the listener.

Use the sounds the poet has given you The poet will have chosen words, not only to convey the meaning through their sense but also through their sound. Let your listeners hear the words with the full value given to the sounds (especially the vowels) and do not rush them or clip them so that their effect is lost. Another poem by Tennyson will illustrate this:

The Eagle

He clasps the crag with crooked hands;
Close to the sun in lonely lands,
Ringed with the azure world, he stands.

The wrinkled sea beneath him crawls:
He watches from his mountain walls,
And like a thunderbolt he falls.

If you read that quickly and do not allow those expressive words to sound – clasps, crag, crooked, lonely, ringed, azure, wrinkled, crawls, thunderbolt, falls – you drain most of the poet's meaning from the lines. Try reading it aloud quite naturally but with sufficient control for the vowels and consonants to be clearly heard and enjoyed and the effect will be quite different. When you recognize that the sounds of a poet's words are as important as their 'dictionary meaning' (are in fact part of the meaning), you will be well on the road to being a good reader of poetry. If the sounds are as important as this, it is a very good argument for speaking poetry aloud rather than keeping it in the silent confines of the printed page.

Convey the rhythm of the lines, but do not let the rhythm dominate. The rhythmic beat of many poems is so obvious that you have little difficulty in discovering it. It is sometimes so insistent that the reader's voice falls into a fatal jog-trot which dominates the whole reading and can even destroy the sense. Very young children are prone to this. They respond so readily to the attractions of the rhythm that nothing else matters. Think how you and your friends used to say (or chant) the nursery rhyme 'A-ring a-ring of roses . . .' That kind of unvarying beat, often accompanied by a sing-song tone, will not do for more advanced verse reading.

The challenge is to allow the rhythmic pattern to come through to the listeners' ears, yet at the same time to integrate it with the sound of normal speech. What you must not do is destroy the poet's rhythm in a rash attempt to make his lines sound 'natural'.

Be aware of the line endings When a poem has a well-marked regular rhythm, the use of lines is obvious. At other times – especially in many modern poems – one line seems to end and another begin for no obvious reason. But the poet will have had a reason for doing this and you must take note of the line-endings in your reading.

There are two ways of misusing the ends of lines: one is to stop dead at each one; the other is to rush over line-endings as if they did not exist or as if the poet was being perverse in not continuing the line up to the margin of the page. Line-endings are to do with the rhythmic pattern of the whole poem and are very often marked by rhyme. When you speak a poem aloud, the listeners' ears will be satisfied if they are kept aware of the pattern and rhyme scheme without having it thumped at them, and without the poem being turned into nonsense by your stopping at the end of each line. Poets often run the sense over from one line to the next with no punctuation at the end of some of the lines, as in this example from Coleridge's famous poem, 'Kubla Khan':

1. In Xanadu did Kubla Khan
2. A stately pleasure-dome decree:
3. Where Alph, the sacred river, ran
4. Through caverns measureless to man
5. Down to a sunless sea.

The tune of the voice must carry over the sense without a break between lines 1 and 2 and then between 3 and 4. Whether you carry over lines 4 to 5 without the slightest of breaks would be your decision. You might need a quick breath at that point and it would not affect the sense as it would if you took a breath between lines 1 and 2 or between 3 and 4. Take care how you 'run over' from one line to the next. Do not spoil the rhythm of the first line through your anxiety to reach the next by hurrying the last word. Lines 3 and 4 should *not* be made to sound:

Where Alph, the sacred river
Ran through caverns measureless to man.

In other words, always give the last word in a line its full rhythmic value, even when (perhaps especially when) you are running one line over to the next.

Audience Awareness

It is very hard *not* to be aware of an audience. Whether you are really enjoying yourself as the centre of attention or wishing you were anywhere on earth except in front of that listening group, you know very well that you have an audience. Yet GCSE assessors are instructed to take note of your 'audience awareness'. This is because it is quite possible to speak in front of a group and totally ignore them!

There are all sorts of ways to do this: you bury your head in a sheaf of notes and never once look the audience in the eyes; you mumble what you are saying to yourself and to no one else; you disregard any reaction from your listeners, whether it be laughter or a yawn; you show an intense interest in your own visual aids, especially those which enable you to turn your back on your audience and talk to the wall. This kind of behaviour may give you a very temporary relief from 'nerves' but the resulting talk, discussion or reading will gain little credit from your listeners – or from the assessors.

The essence of oral English is *communication*. The whole point of speaking, whether to an individual or to a large group, is to gain a response. You may wonder if this is always true: can it apply, for instance, to a Headmaster addressing 500 students in Assembly? It seems a very one-sided activity. But you can be absolutely sure that the Headmaster is keenly aware of all kinds of signals that are coming to him from his audience . . . hushed silence, shuffling feet and wandering eyes, cheerful smiles, sullen frowns, bored inattention or rapt interest. The Head will also be responding to these signals – extending the effect he is making if he feels his audience is with him or hurrying to a close if the hall is becoming restless.

In a similar way, the success of your communication will depend on the response you evoke from the listeners. This is true of a group discussion or an informal conversation as much as of a fully prepared speech to a whole class. An assessor of 'audience awareness' will be looking at precisely this: how sensitive are you to the reactions of your audience, how skilled are you at evoking the response you need for the best communication of your material and how do you modify your own approach in the light of the audience's reactions to you?

The first step in showing an awareness of your listeners is actually to look at them. This seems an obvious remark, but you must know from your own experience how many speakers and readers prefer to look anywhere rather than straight at the audience. Of course the faces of a listening class can be daunting at first, but you cannot communicate effectively if you shut off your personality from your audience and this is what happens if you keep your eyes down or speak to the side walls. Once you allow yourself to look at your listeners, you are quite likely to be cheered by their encouraging smiles or expectant looks as they wait to hear what you are going to say. Do not disappoint them by immediately dropping your eyes or turning away.

Eye-contact is equally important in group discussion. If there are five of you at a table, the ones who look confidently around the group as they put their points forward will be much more effective than those who have their say with eyes focused firmly on the table top.

Another basic courtesy to your listeners is to allow them to hear you. It is amazing how many people, including some who hold important positions in the world, seem incapable of realizing how inaudible they are. If a speaker calls out, 'Can you hear me at the back?' he deserves at least some credit for acknowledging the presence of the audience and showing a desire to be heard by them. Too often such speakers, having shown their apparent willingness to communicate, then relapse into their habitual murmur and contact with the back of the hall is lost. In a classroom you should not be troubled by the vastness of the space where you have to speak, but schools can be noisy places (whether for internal or external reasons) and a clear voice, good diction and a reasonable level of sound will maintain and hold your audience-contact. Your assessor will also consider these purely vocal qualities. More help is given with them in the chapter on 'Clear Speech' (p. 75)

'Audience-awareness' involves *listening*. You may think this is an activity that has to take a back seat when you are giving a talk or are reading aloud but, as with the Headmaster mentioned earlier, there are things you hear when you talk apart from the sound of your own voice. Moreover, when you have finished the talk or reading, then comes the time for questions and discussion; to respond efficiently you have to listen carefully to what is being asked. Nor is it just a matter of being quite sure what your questioner is asking. You need to take account of the *tone* of the question – especially if it seems to challenge something you have said – and then choose a way of replying that not only answers the question but also satisfies the rest of the listeners that you have dealt with the question properly. Incidentally, when replying to a question, make sure that all the audience have heard it (repeat it if necessary) and address your answer to everyone. In other words, do not appear to be having a private conversation with the questioner alone.

In a group discussion 'audience-awareness' is at the very centre of the process. No productive discussion can go forward if each member states his or her own position and has no regard for anyone else in the group. Listening, thinking and contributing means full awareness of everyone else in the discussion. Nothing is more quickly noticed than the member who has no sensitivity to others and is intent on nothing else but forcing his or her own view.

Role-Play

Role-play means improvising speech situations. In effect you are acting a part. You pretend to be someone else in order to find the words to express their emotions and their reactions to certain circumstances. It can be something as businesslike as rehearsing a possible job interview. On the other hand it can be an imaginative exercise, such as improvising a speech that Frankenstein's Monster might have made in Mary Shelley's famous novel – but didn't. Whatever the source of the improvisation, it involves the devising of appropriate language and therefore is an admirable English activity and one that can be assessed as part of GCSE course work.

To be successful in role-play you have to use your imagination and use it sensitively and sympathetically. In order to speak the words of a harassed mother arguing with her teenage son, or a young man desperately trying to talk himself into a job, you have to try to put yourself into that person's place. You will need to give the assignment some preliminary thought, even if only a few minutes is allowed for this. Use the time to picture your character as clearly as you can: the clothes being worn, the room where the action is happening and as much personal detail as you can think of – age, appearance, class, home background and attitude to life. All these can affect the kind of language such a character would use. A mother from an upper-middle-class family would use language in talking to her son that would differ in various ways from that used by a poor woman. The value and interest of role-play is to explore these differences and to see whether the language represents a difference in the quality of the feeling or only in the social circumstances. To make your improvisation as convincing as possible you have to use your imagination, based on your experience of how people behave and speak. Central to this is imagining the emotions and attitudes of the people you are portraying. This must come first, because language will flow from these feelings and not vice-verse.

There is no need to feel you must be a highly skilled actor to succeed in this. GCSE English is not an examination in acting. All the same, if you can match your words with an accent and tone of voice which help to bring to life the character you are improvising, so much the better.

The ability to use several kinds of speech appropriate to different situations is one we all possess naturally to a greater or lesser extent. You no doubt speak to a head teacher in a way quite different from the way you talk to a fellow student. There would be differences between the language you used to a policeman and to a vicar; to a boy or girl friend and to your grandmother. The technical name for these different kinds of language is *register*. GCSE assessors expect you to show an awareness of this and the ability to use the appropriate register for whatever speech situation you are in. Role-play is excellent practice for trying out different registers.

A possible source of role-play is your English Literature course. To understand the motivation of a character in a novel or play it is sometimes rewarding to become that person for a few minutes in an improvisation. Some classes, when they study a scene from Shakespeare, enact the basic situation in their own words and in a modern setting in order to confront the issue in contemporary terms. For example, a worker belonging to a different racial group from all his workmates may be made to feel an outsider until one of them wants to borrow money from him. How the request is made and how the lonely man reacts provide good material for role-play and for considering the issues – and the language used – in a way we can immediately understand. Then the class turn to Shakespeare and see how he presented a similar situation with Shylock, the Jew in *The Merchant of Venice*.

Situations from novels can also be explored in this way in your own words. It is also interesting to improvise the scenes that an author chose *not* to write, filling out in your own way events and conversations that are mentioned in the story but not described in detail. Whenever you study works of literature using this method, it is important to return to the book afterwards, for it is the author's work – and words – that are your prime concern. Such role-play, however, helps to sharpen your awareness and increase your involvement in the book or play you are reading.

Telephoning

One form of role-play that will often be part of an improvised scene is telephoning. This is also excellent training for real life, since most of us these days frequently use the telephone. Ideally you require a pair of practice telephones through which you really can talk to a partner on the other side of the room. But if these are not available, you and your partner can sit with your backs to each other a few feet apart, holding 'invisible' phones to your ears.

In improvising a domestic phone conversation – say between two housewives – you would try to capture the informality of their talk. But if you were making a business call, you would have to be much more precise in what you said, especially if you were representing a commercial firm. There is a great deal to learn about efficient telephoning but here are some basic hints:

If you are the caller

1. Always have a note-pad and pencil to hand before you begin the call.
2. Decide in advance precisely what you are ringing up about. If your business is at all complicated, then write down beforehand the points you want to discuss.
3. Ask clearly for the person to whom you wish to speak, either by name or by position (e.g. 'May I speak to Mr Jones please?' or 'May I speak to the Sales Manager please?').
4. When that person is on the line, identify yourself and state your business briefly and to the point.
5. If you are given information, such as an instruction to follow or an address to contact, write it down on your pad.
6. Repeat back information you have received in order to make sure you have taken it down accurately.
7. If you think you may have to follow up this conversation with a further call, inquire the name of the person to whom you are speaking – and write it down.

8. If you have a number of points to discuss, warn the person receiving the call of this early on, so that he or she does not ring off before you have raised all you wanted to.
9. Spell out difficult words – as in name and address, for instance – and speak numbers particularly slowly and clearly.
10. At the end of the call express thanks for the help you have received and ring off politely.

If you are receiving the call

1. Make sure you have a note-pad and pencil to hand.
2. Identify your firm and department and, if you wish, use some such phrase as 'Can I help you?'
   (e.g. 'Good morning. Smith and Bloggs Ltd. Can I help you?')
   It is better to avoid the casual greeting 'Hello'.
3. When the caller has announced his or her business, politely inquire the caller's name and write it down. Thereafter use the caller's name in the conversation where possible.
4. Unless it is very straightforward, make a note of what the caller is asking. This is for your own use and, more especially, if you have to pass the information on to someone else (your employer perhaps).
5. If you have to find the information elsewhere, ask the caller either to hold the line or else offer to call him or her back when you know the answer.
6. If there is to be any follow-up, ask for the caller's name and address and telephone number and write them down. Check these back to make sure you have written them down correctly.
7. Repeat back any other information you may have received to ensure you have not misunderstood or mis-copied anything.
8. Remain calm and polite even if the person at the other end is becoming abusive and angry.
9. For the sake of your firm's reputation, avoid slang and casual remarks – especially 'OK'.
10. Bring the conversation to an end courteously and, if appropriate, thank the person for calling.

Clear Speech

Your GCSE oral assessment is based on the way you communicate your thoughts. But there can be no effective communication if your words cannot be heard clearly by other people. That is why each Examination Group requires your teacher-assessors to take into consideration such purely vocal qualities as clear diction and the pace, pitch, and intonation of your delivery. However good your ideas are and however well expressed in words, you will not score as highly as you might if you speak indistinctly and never raise your voice above a monotonous mumble.

Probably your voice is perfectly adequate for your private conversations and other day-to-day needs. But when you use it in serious discussions to exchange ideas or to get things done, it has to be audible and immediately intelligible. When you are giving a talk to a group, large or small, or are presenting a reading, you have to make sure your voice is reaching the audience and enabling them to listen to you with interest and pleasure – and not with annoyance at the indistinctness of your speech.

None of us can do other than use the voice we already have and which has developed through our childhood and adolescence. There is no point in being in any way ashamed of your natural voice or self-conscious about it. It is very much part of you and of your personality and is capable of doing most of the things you want it to do for you in everyday life. It may well have more good qualities than you recognize. On the other hand, you may have to be honest with yourself and admit that you do not always speak as clearly as you could and that your communication would be all the better for a little practice in voice technique. Before we make some suggestions to help you with this, let's clear the ground about one point that often troubles people: will it matter in GCSE if you have a local accent?

Your accent

The answer to that question is a very definite no! What the new examination wants to encourage is lively, natural speech – and for you that means the speech natural to you and the area you live in. No one expects you to change your local accent for the purposes of the examination into that used by BBC announcers. The key phrase is 'effective communication' and you will communicate most effectively with your fellow students and with your teachers in the local accent with which you are all familiar. In some cases this will be characteristic of the region of the country in which you live, of a big city or a remote country area. In other schools most people will speak in an accent not much different from the standard accent of the BBC. No single accent will be considered superior to another by the assessors. What you have to aim for is clarity *within your own accent*, together with all the desirable vocal qualities of interesting variety of tone, liveliness, vigour and audibility. Only if your accent is a barrier to effective communication should you be concerned about it. This might occur if you left your area and went to a different part of the country. It could also be a problem if your job, when you left school, took you among people who expected to hear a different accent. But as far as GCSE oral examinations are concerned, you can confidently use the accent that comes most naturally to you.

Check points

We are so used to the sounds of our own voices and to our own ways of speaking that we cannot always recognize our own faults. A friend who would comment honestly (but tactfully) on your speech would be invaluable. If you have to carry out the check for yourself, here are some areas to assess:

Audibility Are you speaking loudly enough to be heard? In a group discussion with four other people sitting in a small circle you will of course need far less volume than if you are addressing a room full of people. In fact a booming voice in a small group situation is very off-putting, but so is a weak voice in a very large hall. It is all a matter of being sensitive to your audience and to the circumstances: room size, extraneous noise, attitude of listeners and so on. Very often people speak too quietly out of shyness or nerves. If you are going to contribute to a discussion or give a talk, then you have to convince yourself that what you have to say is worth hearing – and then make sure that people hear it! It really is a matter of confidence.

Diction There is a natural human tendency to take the easy way out and this is as true about speech as about anything else. If people can convey the sense of words by moving their lips, tongues and jaws as little as possible, then they will do so. It is partly to do with national characteristics: some speakers of other languages seem to use considerable vocal energy while English speakers have for a long time been known for their casual articulation. The Englishman's stiff upper lip is famous and does not do much for clear articulation. Today the older generation are prone to criticize the sloppy speech of their children. But what do they mean by 'sloppy'? Almost certainly they mean a blurring of the distinction between one word and the next, a lack of feeling for the shape of each word and for the difference between one sound and another. If you have been criticized for sloppy speech, poor diction, or whatever phrase was used, try this: choose a short and easy sentence such as 'Today the sun is shining brightly', and say it slowly and deliberately, but without breaking its natural-sounding rhythm. As you speak it, think of each word in turn *as a word* and say each as clearly as you can. Make the consonants (t, th, s, n, sh, br, l) very distinct – especially the t in 'brightly' – and each vowel well shaped. Then bring the pace up to normal speed and see if you can keep the same clarity. If you are really keen to improve your diction, then you will need to devise and practise such exercises regularly. Here are some more phrases to improve the articulation of certain consonants:

Pick up the book. Pack the box and put it away.
Tear the end of the ticket. Don't take down the tins.
Get a good kick at it. Can't you be good and kind?
Fill five vans with furs. Various vessels fell to the floor.
The thieves gather around the thicket. They loathe those who thieve.

The fisherman mends his nets. She measured the length and breadth of the kitchen.
The old jewel was folded in rolled gold.

When you have made your lips and tongue work efficiently to produce neat and clear consonants, go over the above sentences once more, giving special thought to the *vowel* sounds within the words. Make sure they are well-shaped and distinct.

Pitch The level at which you create your speech (i.e. low, medium or high in musical terms) affects both the audibility and the interest of what you are saying. A high shrill voice quickly becomes unpleasant and a very low-pitched voice tends to be difficult to hear clearly. Both become boring after a short time. Of these two, it is more common to find a voice pitched too low for easy audibility. If you want to gain attention in a discussion or in a talk, it is a good idea to pitch your voice a very little higher than usual when you begin to speak. Of course whatever pitch you adopt initially will be varied by the natural rise and fall of your voice as you speak. Allow this natural variety full play. People become dull speakers when they iron out the rise and fall of speech tunes so that they are virtually using only one pitch. That is called a 'monotone', which leads inevitably to – monotony.

Pace When you join in a group discussion, you are not likely to worry much about the pace of your delivery. You will be concentrating on the remarks you want to contribute. All the same, your colleagues will be reacting to your pace. You will be spoiling the effect of what you want to say if you make all your remarks in a breathless rush or drag them out of yourself with agonizing slowness. The pace will be even more important if you are giving a talk. If you hurry, the listeners will not be able to take everything in; if you are ponderous, they will grow bored. As in all oral activity, you have to be sensitive to your audience and adapt the speed of your delivery to what seems right for those listeners at the time.

Paying attention to these four check points – audibility, diction, pitch and pace – is well worth doing, but when all is said and done, good delivery will very much depend on your own wish to communicate effectively and on having the confidence to try. If you are enthusiastic about what you want to communicate and eager to share it with others, your speech is likely to be lively, vigorous and compelling. It will be all the better for your attention to the diction and other technical matters, but the essential thing is your own desire to communicate. The two sides interact. If you develop clear speech and a pleasing voice, these will give you confidence to share your ideas: if you have ideas and interests you want to share, then you will be encouraged to make your own voice an effective means of communication.

The Last Word

'STOP TALKING!' That command has rung through thousands of classrooms, but it is going to sound increasingly out of place in future. Naturally a teacher requires silence so that instructions can be heard and information imparted. The ability to *listen* quietly is something we all need to cultivate, for there can be little learning without it. But an English class in which there is no purposeful talk except from the teacher is these days regarded as a failure. The GCSE oral assessments recognize this, and the syllabuses are designed to make that kind of English teaching a thing of the past.

You now have the chance of using in class the kind of language you will most frequently employ throughout your life – spoken language. Accept the opportunity offered to you by being prepared to speak in class and contribute orally to its activities. The reward will be much more than a good grade in GCSE oral English . . .